HISTORIC  SCOT

ANCIENT
SHETLAND

For David, and our family
In memory of Sheila Mary Marsh (1932–96)
and Pamela June Turner (1925–97)

HISTORIC SCOTLAND

ANCIENT SHETLAND

VAL TURNER

B. T. Batsford Ltd / Historic Scotland

Typeset by Bernard Cavender Design & Greenwood Graphics Publishing
and printed by The Bath Press, Bath

Published by B. T. Batsford Ltd
583 Fulham Road, London SW6 5BY

A CIP catalogue record for this book is
available from the British Library.

ISBN 0 7134 8000 9 (limp)
ISBN 0 7134 8001 7 (cased)

(Front cover) Mousa Broch (Historic Scotland)
(Back cover) Bone Comb from Upper Scalloway (Niall Sharples)

Contents

Illustrations

Colour plates

(Between pages 64 and 65)

Acknowledgements

As I write this book, Shetland is in the midst of a ferment of archaeological research. The results of previous excavations, some undertaken as long as twenty years ago, are in the process of being brought to publication and a tide of new research is under way. Shetland Amenity Trust has had an important role to play as a catalyst in much of this, often in partnership with Historic Scotland. The disadvantage of writing at such a time is that our rapidly expanding understanding of Shetland's past will inevitably alter what we currently believe to be true. But to delay for such reasons could be to delay for ever!

In order to make this book an up-to-the minute account of what we know about Shetland's past, I have had wide-ranging discussions with many friends and colleagues. Several of them have generously allowed me access to unpublished reports and have helped to shape my thoughts. While any errors are my own, I must acknowledge a debt of gratitude to Patrick Ashmore, Julie Bond, Kate Canter, Mike Canter, Stephen Carter, Steve Dockrill, Jane Downes, Noel Fojut, Katherine Forsyth, Steffen Stumman Hansen, John Hunter, Raymond Lamb, Anne-Christine Larsen, Olwyn Owen, Hazel Moore, Jimmy Moncrieff, Paul Sharman, Dave Starley, Niall Sharples, Ian Simpson, Brian Smith, Bruce Walker and Graeme Wilson. Joanna Richards has done a marvellous job of turning my thoughts into reconstruction drawings, and I am deeply indebted to her for her patience and attention to detail. Anna Purdy has helped in many ways, particularly in producing several of the maps and diagrams, and Catrina MacInnes saved me considerable time by typing the first draft. David Breeze, series editor, Jackie Henrie and Pauline Marsh, copy-editors, have given me great assistance in tightening my script. Jim Keddie and Laurence Malcolmson built a dry-stone dyke outside my window while I wrote the text and, by discussion and demonstration, helped me to see archaeological structures through their eyes. Special thanks are due to Brian Smith, Jimmy Moncrieff and David Marsh, all of whom read the text and offered valuable advice, spiced with humour. Above all, the practical help and forbearance of David, together with those of many of my friends, have given me the time and space which I needed to complete the task. I hope that I've done justice to them all.

In addition to Joanna Richards' marvellous reconstruction drawings (11,17, 28, 36, 37, 40, 44, 54, 64, 66, 71), I should like to thank Historic Scotland (1, 6, 14, 16, 23, 27, 43, 46, 50, 51, 53, 48, 65, **colour plates 6, 8, 13**) Shetland Museum (10, 18, 19, 25, 30, 31, 35, **colour plates 2, 4, 7**) Shetland Amenity Trust (8, 75, **colour plates 1, 3, 14 (a) and (b)**, National Museums of Scotland (15, 67, 68, 69, 70, 72, colour plate 11) RCAHMS (12, 22, 29, 33, 39, 42, 45, 47, 55, 57) Alasdair Whittle (9, 21,) Niall Sharples (52, colour plate 9) Deborah Lamb (colour plate 5) Rod McCullough (49) J C R Hamilton (74) Steve Dockrill (colour plate 15) for allowing me to reproduce their photographs and Anna Purdy for drawing illustrations for me (2, 3, 7, 13, 34, 41, 56, 58, 60, 61, 62, 63). The remainder of the photographs and illustrations are my own.

1
The Old Rock

Shetland is probably the most exciting place in Britain for the average person to discover archaeology for themselves. It offers dramatic individual monuments, including Mousa Broch, which stands 13m (43ft) high, and spectacular multi-period sites, such as Jarlshof (1), where some of the remains of the 4000 years represented stand to their original heights. At both of these monuments visitors can climb to the top, or crawl through passages or around cells or souterrains. Each visitor can have their own experience of being able to discover the past for themselves.

More remarkable still is the fact that Shetland has large tracts of prehistoric landscape which have survived virtually intact for 2000–3000 years. At the southern end of Shetland this is the result of blown sand which concealed and protected earlier landscapes from succeeding generations. Elsewhere, early prehistoric settlers carved fields and territories from the hillsides, and built houses and burial cairns amongst them. Some of these settlements lasted for over 1000 years, but, whether because of soil

1 Jarlshof (Historic Scotland)

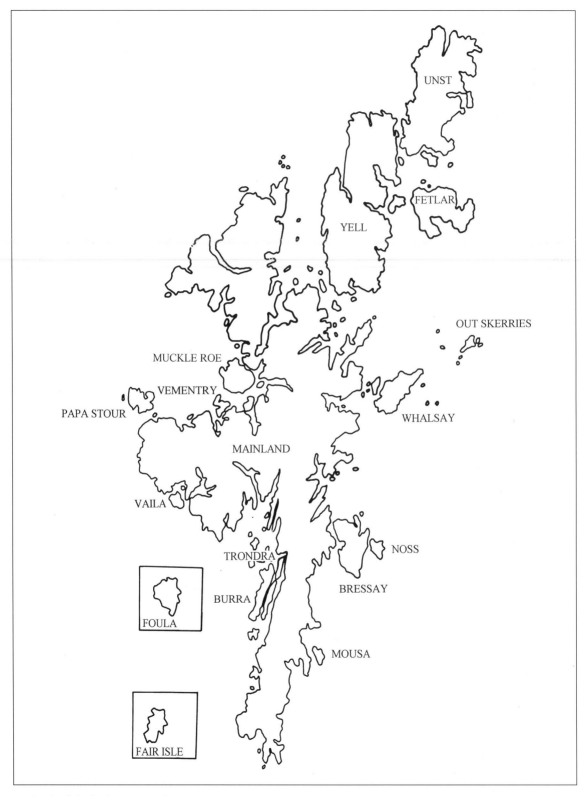

2 Islands of Shetland. (Anna Purdy)

exhaustion, climatic deterioration, or a combination of the two, they were eventually engulfed by blanket peat which spread down from the hilltops and encroached from boggy hollows. Much of the higher agricultural land was either reduced to grazing or abandoned completely. Since then the hills have been used fairly continuously for grazing, primarily for sheep but also for Shetland ponies. Fortunately for archaeology, prehistoric Shetlanders often built in stone which was both readily available and durable. As a result, prehistoric boundaries can be traced for miles as the larger building stones still protrude through the peat. The West Side of Mainland Shetland is one of the best areas for seeing this. In other areas, remains are concealed by deeper peat, and may only be discovered as a result of peat cutting or erosion.

The Old Rock

The 'Old Rock', as Shetland is sometimes affectionately known, is an archipelago of over 500 islands, eighteen of which are inhabited today (2). In the past, most of them were either inhabited or at least used for pasture, even if this involved shipping animals to them by boat on a seasonal basis or forcing animals to swim

out. In previous generations, the sea united rather than divided, and it was a positive advantage that nowhere in Shetland is (with sea level at today's height) more than 5km (3 miles) from the sea.

Shetland is situated further north than is generally realized (3). In reality, most of the islands lie between 60° and 62° north, at the same latitude as Bergen, Helsinki, Siberia and southern Greenland. This places Shetland in the middle of the Atlantic seaways, where the North Sea and the Atlantic Ocean meet; a position which has had a significant impact on the islands throughout time. During recent centuries, as transport has become increasingly land-based and Shetland has been governed from the United Kingdom, so the islands have increasingly become regarded as peripheral and difficult of access.

Geology

The overall appearance of Shetland is long and thin. The islands are composed of the tops of a ridge of submerged hills aligned north–south, part of the ridge which separated the Atlantic

3 Location of Shetland. (after Morrison) (Anna Purdy)

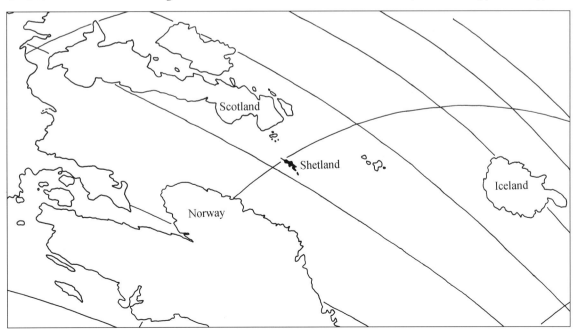

Ocean from the North Sea, and which extends from Fair Isle in the south to Unst in the north and continues on to Faroe. Shetland Mainland measures 96km (60 miles) north–south, but is only 32km (20 miles) across at its widest point. The voes (long inlets of sea) and upland ridges follow the north–south alignment.

The geology of Shetland is very complex. The bedrock is largely igneous and metamorphic (**4**). Sandstone outcrops to the south and west. In prehistoric times sandstone lent itself to a variety of stone tools, from plough shares (ard points) to pounders. Flagstone in the South Mainland, Mousa and Bressay made good building stone, as well as being suitable for making slate knives, 'pot lids' and even gaming boards! A limestone strip surfaces in the Central

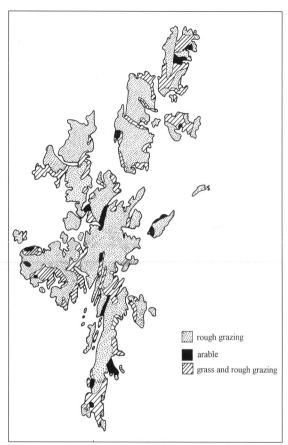

5 Land capability in Shetland. (Val Turner)

rough grazing

arable

grass and rough grazing

Catagories of bedrock

sedimentary

intrusive igneous

metamorphic

volcanic

4 Simplified geology of Shetland. (Val Turner)

Mainland (Whiteness, Tingwall and South Nesting) and has created a band of good agricultural land. The basic rocks underlying the islands of Unst and Fetlar (the 'Garden of Shetland') in the north also create fertile soils on what is some of the flattest land (**5**). Most of the land, however, is not fertile; the granites of Muckle Roe and Ronas Hill and the volcanic rocks of Papa Stour and Eshaness create dramatic scenery but do not encourage agriculture.

The islands are rich in minerals. There is copper in Fair Isle and in Vidlin; soapstone (steatite or talc) is found in numerous small outcrops from Fetlar and Unst in the north to Cunningsburgh in the south; there is even gold (in minute quantities) in Unst! In Neolithic times soapstone was ground down and incorporated into pottery, while glacial deposits of clay provided the other essential ingredient. Quartz was used in lieu of flint to make arrowheads and scrapers and felsite was used to make the beautiful 'Shetland knives' (see Chapter 4).

Physical geography

Shetland is not particularly rugged. The highest point, Ronas Hill, is only 453m (1486ft) above present sea level. The vegetation on Ronas Hill is, however, tundra: a salutary reminder of Shetland's latitude. The surface of the hill is very fragile; the flora is Arctic-alpine in character, and includes miniature willow less than 2cm (1in) high.

The islands were heavily glaciated during the last Ice Age, giving rise to the wide fertile valleys of Tingwall and Dales Lees in Shetland Mainland and creating hollows, which are now occupied by small lochs, in the north and west of the Mainland. The ice also scored deep valleys, some of which were subsequently drowned by the sea and softened by erosion and silting. As a result, 'voes' project into the land. The voes are flanked by relatively flat land, often taken into cultivation, and are protected from the worst excesses of a stormy sea. Inland the ice gave rise to numerous small lochs, bogs and burns – an abundance of water! Other effects of glaciation have been disguised by subsequent erosion and the growth of peat. At Sandy Loch, near Lerwick, the peat is over 6m (20ft) deep, and the island of Yell has the unwarranted reputation of being a blanket bog 27km (17 miles) long! As early as the Neolithic period, people had discovered the value of peat as a fuel (a discovery sometimes erroneously attributed to the Viking Torf Einar).

Only 50km (30 miles) north-west of Shetland the European continental shelf ends and the seabed drops away dramatically. During the last glaciation the ice sheet pressed down on Scotland, causing it to sink under the weight; Shetland, at the edge of the continental shelf, began to rise. Once the ice began to melt, the pressure on Scotland lifted, and it began to rise again, so causing Shetland to sink. As a result,

the sea level around Shetland has been rising at the rate of about 1m (3ft) per 1000 years. In areas where the land is gently shelving, such as in parts of the South Mainland and on the island of Unst, a metre in height would make a significant difference to the amount of land above sea level. The rising sea level impedes drainage and may inundate settlement in low-lying valleys.

The power of the sea also causes sand and shingle to move about constantly. A strip of sand, or tombola, links St Ninian's Isle to the Mainland, and there are sand bars in several other bays such as Dales Voe, near Toft. Blown sand has been a mixed blessing at Jarlshof and Quendale, both in the South Mainland; in small quantities it acts as a fertilizer, but in excess it buries both farmland and houses – although at Jarlshof and nearby at Old Scatness this has been to the benefit of archaeologists.

In areas where the coast is formed by cliffs, the constant battering of the sea has resulted in large landfalls and steep cliffs. At 200m (655ft) the cliffs of Foula are the highest sea cliffs in Britain. It is virtually impossible to predict a route of coastal erosion for any given place; in Nesting a few years ago an entire lighthouse disappeared overnight, when the cliff on which it was standing collapsed into the sea!

Climate

Given Shetland's latitude it is fortunate that it lies in the path of the Gulf Stream which keeps its winters as mild as those of London, with an annual average of only fifteen mornings of snow. Shetland's summers, however, remain cool. Being exposed, in the Atlantic, the islands are also subject to violent storms and have an average of fifty-eight days per year on which the wind is at least gale force. Strong winds and driving rain cause both soil and coastal erosion. The winds carry salt which stunts plants, and nowhere is far enough from the sea to be exempt. They also carry sand and shell fragments which in moderation can lighten the soil.

Latitude also affects the hours of sunlight which Shetland receives. The midwinter sun is below the horizon for eighteen hours, and on an overcast day it seems never to get light, but at the 'Simmer Dim' (midsummer) there is virtually no night. The long summer days help to counteract some of the problems of a short growing season, although the angle of the sun is so low that its energy is diffused. There is also a substantial amount of summer fog and cloud; as a result the risk of crop failure would have been an ever-present threat in prehistoric times. Shetland's growing season at sea level is the same as that at 350m (1150ft) above sea level in the central Highlands. Today, this is reflected in the upland sheep subsidy, which classifies upland Shetland as starting at sea level. The land is considered to be 'severely disadvantaged'. Not surprisingly, the archaeology of ancient Shetland is both upland and rural in character.

Nature's larder

Shetlanders have long been described as 'fishermen with crofts'. There are no land mammals indigenous to Shetland. Red deer, cattle and sheep were all brought in by settlers; even the otter was probably introduced. Without the rich resources of the sea, settlement would have been an unattractive proposition. Seals and the occasional whale provided meat, oil for light, bone for tools, and skin for clothing. Shellfish could be eaten or used as bait to catch bigger fish, either from the shore or from small boats. Seaweed may have supplemented the diet, as well as providing fertilizer for the early farmers.

The abundant bird population would also have contributed to a subsistence diet. Flocks of nesting sea-birds would have been easy to catch during the summer months, and seasonally available eggs would have made a welcome addition to the diet. During spring and autumn migrating birds would have come ashore, often exhausted and therefore easy prey. The evidence from Jarlshof suggests that sea-birds were a regular part of the diet.

Herbs, berries and insects would have supplemented an essentially seafood diet. Some of these may also have had medicinal properties. Ancient Shetlanders would have known far more about which roots, fungi, shoots, leaves, seeds, nuts and bugs were good to eat than we do today.

The history of Shetland's archaeology

As long ago as the middle of the eighteenth century, travellers such as George Low (1774) wrote about the places which they visited, commenting on what they saw and even carrying out their own investigations. At the Broch of Houlland, in Eshaness, Low 'pulled down … part of the wall in search of any cement (and) found none'. John Tudor's travelogue of 1883 describes prominent sites such as Clickhimin Broch and Scalloway Castle.

In 1878, with varying degrees of success, the Ordnance Survey compiled the *Original Name Books* for Shetland, in an attempt to list local place-names and spellings. Monuments were also described and recorded on the First Edition maps. The Ordnance Survey continued to update this information, adding large numbers of new sites as recently as the 1960s.

During the late nineteenth century, there was a proliferation of interest in archaeological sites in Shetland. The archaeologist Gilbert Goudie carried out several excavations. In July 1888 he supervised the clearance of stone from the Broch of Clumlie, which he continued during 1890 and 1891 with a grant from the Society of Antiquaries of Scotland. In 1895 and 1896 this led to a six-month debate in the letters page of the *Shetland News* concerning the origin of the 'Pictish Towers'. The correspondence began with a discussion as to whether Clumlie was Celtic or Scandinavian in origin.

At the end of the nineteenth century a series of violent storms began to accelerate the erosion of the peninsula on which Jarlshof stands. Between 1897 and 1905, the owner of the site, Mr John Bruce, undertook an excavation, during which he explored the broch and two wheelhouses. In 1925 the Ministry of Works acquired the site, which was then excavated by Alexander Curle and Professor Gordon Childe. The Second World War held up the work for ten years, after which John Hamilton completed the task (**6**).

In the early 1930s the Royal Commission on the Ancient and Historical Monuments of Scotland sent John Corrie to Shetland with a brief to record the sites which the Ordnance Survey had noted. Although he filled eight notebooks with local information and observations about the archaeology, Corrie realized that work of a far larger scale was required. By 1934 Corrie's health was failing, and Charles Calder came to Shetland to finish the task. Calder was all too well aware of the limitations of the exercise and determined to come back at a later date. Like the work of Curle and Childe at Jarlshof, the compilation of the Royal Commission *Inventory* was also hindered by the war. It was finally published in 1946, eight years after Corrie's death. For forty years the *Inventory* provided a basic framework for work in Shetland.

In the 1950s Charles Calder returned, primarily in order to record the previously ignored oval

houses. He also excavated at Stanydale and Gruting School on the West Side, and at Pettigarth's Field in Whalsay. In 1958 a small excavation led by Professor O'Dell of Aberdeen University attracted attention when twenty-eight pieces of Pictish silver, the St Ninian's Isle Treasure, was uncovered. In 1966 a purpose-built museum was constructed in Lerwick to house the treasure, but this was not to be. The finds were declared 'Treasure Trove' in 1963 following lengthy legal wrangles as to whether or not udal law should be applied (twelfth-century Norse law which would have divided the treasure equally between the finder, the landowner and the Crown). Nevertheless, Shetlanders still believed that once they had a purpose-built museum with special security cases for the treasure, it would be returned to Shetland. It never has, and so remains in Edinburgh, whilst the replicas of the silver are on display in the Shetland Museum. The court case itself was also significant because it confirmed that the law of Treasure Trove applies to non-precious objects: the silver was found together with the jaw-bone of a porpoise.

6 Excavation at Jarlshof in 1952. (Historic Scotland)

The establishment of a museum led to the founding of an Archaeological and Natural History Society, which undertook several excavations up to 1975. Further work, much of which was at the behest of and sponsored by Historic Scotland, was carried out by a number of excavators during the 1970s and early 1980s. In 1986 Shetland Amenity Trust created the post of 'Shetland Archaeologist'. Today, the Shetland Sites and Monuments Record, held at the Trust, contains details of over 5000 sites and is being added to almost daily. The last ten years have seen major advances in both the techniques of archaeology and the amount of work carried out in Shetland. In the following chapters I will try to synthesize the results of this exciting work.

2
Mesolithic Shetland?

There were Mesolithic people in the Western Isles as early as 6500 BC; indeed, the earliest date for settlement in Scotland comes from the island of Rhum. Dug-out canoes of this period have been found at several places throughout Europe, and early rock carvings from Scandinavia suggest that people knew how to make boats by stretching skins over a wooden frame. Travellers could have minimized the dangers of travelling by sea by keeping close to the shore and always travelling to visible points of land. If Mesolithic people came to Shetland from mainland Scotland or the Western Isles, they could have kept land in view all the way to Shetland. (A return journey would have been more difficult, as the northern islands of Orkney are too flat to be visible from Fair Isle.) Nevertheless, the journey from the north of Orkney would have been daunting because travellers would have had to venture across open sea, negotiating potentially treacherous currents such as the tide race at Sumburgh Roost.

Until recently, scholars believed that Mesolithic people did not get to the Northern Isles, and the pollen evidence is not conclusive. Recent work in Orkney, however, has brought to light several sites with Mesolithic artefacts, so demonstrating that Mesolithic people had the capability to travel by sea. Some of the Orcadian objects were found in existing collections; others were found as a result of field walking (a systematic search). Orkney shares Shetland's problem of submerged coasts, and if

Mesolithic sites can be found in Orkney it may only be a matter of time before Mesolithic inland camps are found in Shetland. The abundance of peat will hamper the search, but pollen analysis may help to direct it.

The last Ice Age ended about 10,000 years ago, and 1000 years later the temperature in Shetland would have been similar to that of today. By the time another 1000 years had passed the temperatures may have been as much as 3°C higher (7). On mainland Britain, forests were becoming well established. Shetland, which was much more exposed, supported a light covering of woodland in areas less than 200m (656ft) above present sea level.

As the woodland became established, birch became the most common tree in Shetland; it can tolerate a wide range of conditions and is usually the first tree to become established in any area. Hazel, willow, rowan and juniper, trees which are also usually quick to colonize an area, became established. Oak, alder and elm may have grown in some places, although never in any great numbers. Ferns and tall herbs grew amongst the trees; bog and marsh plants took root in poorly drained soils. Above the tree line the heaths and montane grasslands were species-rich. Birds could come and go from Shetland, but the distances between the islands and mainland Scotland were too great for mammals to swim, so for about 3000 years Shetland was a land dominated by trees, shrubs and birds.

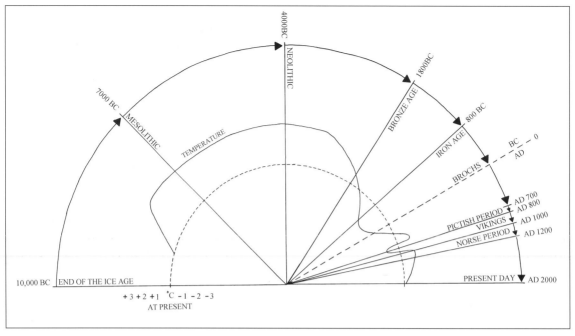

The diagram shows the following labels:

4000BC NEOLITHIC

7000 BC MESOLITHIC

TEMPERATURE

1800BC

BRONZE AGE

800 BC

IRON AGE

BROCHS

BC — 0
AD

AD 700
PICTISH PERIOD AD 800
VIKINGS AD 1000
NORSE PERIOD AD 1200

PRESENT DAY AD 2000

10,000 BC END OF THE ICE AGE

+ 3 + 2 + 1 °C − 1 − 2 − 3
AT PRESENT

7 Time line and temperature fluctuations. (Anna Purdy)

Yet, in some places at least, there seem to have been interruptions to this idyllic picture. Around 5500 BC the pollen record indicates a decline in the juniper, ferns, crowberry and meadowsweet growing around Dallican Water, in Lunnasting. This may have been caused by grazing animals. Mesolithic people lived by hunting prey and gathering food from the woodlands. In other parts of Scotland red deer were a regular part of the diet. For this reason it has been suggested that the 'grazing animals' from Dallican Water were red deer, brought in by Mesolithic incomers. During the same period there was an increase in the amount of microscopic flecks of charcoal in the soil, which might have been caused by Mesolithic settlers making fires (8).

Charcoal in the soil might be derived from cooking meat at a kill site, but a group of people may only have remained in the area until such time as a carcass was used up. Since folk would probably have slept in tents made from branches and skins, the chances of discovering any remains will be low, but they may have left some signs behind them: perhaps a cache of tools left by accident, discarded worn-out scrapers, or debris from making tools. Weapons might have been lost in the hunt: perhaps a spear tip or arrowhead which missed its mark and was never retrieved. As there is no indigenous flint in Shetland, quartz was the best stone available for making blades. It can be very difficult to decide whether or not quartz has been worked, and so chance finds might be easily overlooked.

8 In order to retrieve pollen grains for analysis from excavated sites, the soil has to be 'washed' in a floatation tank. (Shetland Amenity Trust)

20

Traces of Mesolithic settlements might still be found inland in Shetland, perhaps in the few valleys where silt subsequently accumulated, such as Aith's Voe. Inland settlements are only likely to be found by chance, although researchers have been examining the sediments from this particular voe. Further inland the pollen record from sites like Dallican Water will give archaeologists clues as to where to look.

Mesolithic people lived a nomadic life, usually around the coasts, sleeping either in caves or in temporary shelters, as they moved about, following their prey. If they were living in Shetland they would have been heavily dependent on the resources of the sea, and Mesolithic settlement elsewhere in Scotland is generally found along the coast. As sea level in Shetland has risen by as much as 5m (16ft) since the first disturbance to the vegetation at Dallican Water around 5500 BC, any traces of

Mesolithic shelters, tools or middens close to the coast will have disappeared long ago, which may explain why no Mesolithic settlements have ever been found in Shetland. Beaches will have been drowned and caves will have crumbled into the sea.

By about 3450 BC, the woodland at Dallican Water had regenerated as if it had never been disturbed. Perhaps the grazing animals had been hunted to extinction, or perhaps people had either left the area or died out. Whatever the reason, the pollen record demonstrates that until 4000–5000 years ago new woodland could become established in Shetland spontaneously.

Dallican Water is not the only site in Shetland where we know that woodland was lost and then re-established before Shetland began to be farmed. Brunatwatt and the Scord of Brouster, both on the West Side, demonstrate a similar phenomenon.

3
The first farmers

The earliest radiocarbon date for archaeological remains in Shetland is about 3500 BC and comes from beneath a field wall found at Shurton Brae near Lerwick. At the start of this period, Shetland was lightly wooded and the climate was rather warmer than it is today. As a result the land could support more agriculture and could be worked at a higher altitude than at present.

By 3500 BC farming had probably been established in Shetland for at least 500 years. There are no known house sites as early as this, but the earliest farmers may well have lived in wooden houses. Excavation at the Scord of Brouster, on the West Side, revealed the remains of wooden buildings which may have been either temporary shelters or more permanent houses which left little trace. The earliest wooden structure was in use while the land around was being cleared of scrub. Further timber buildings may still lie hidden under the peat. The timber buildings were later replaced by a sequence of three stone buildings. By the time the tombs and houses of the Neolithic (or New Stone Age) farmers appear in the archaeological record, both these and their styles of pottery are distinctively different from the rest of Britain.

An early farm
The Scord of Brouster, on the West Side, is the most complete excavation carried out to date of a prehistoric farm in Shetland (**9**). Today the settlement resembles a village with three stone houses. In reality, it represents over 1500 years of activity, and it is probable that only one house was ever in use at any one time.

The houses were surrounded by six irregularly shaped fields, of about 2.5ha (6 acres) each. These fields probably also evolved over a long period. Two of the houses had field walls attached to them, implying that in each case the field wall was later than the house. Large stones in the bases of some of the field walls may have formed earlier field boundaries. The walls were used as linear clearance cairns, and even the houses had piles of cleared stone thrown up against their walls. Within the fields there are more than 100 clearance cairns which seem to have been constructed in a similar way to the field walls. The similarity between the field walls and cairns suggests that they were roughly contemporary, although both were added to over a long period. The soils must have been either eroded or poorly developed before the permanent fields were created for stone clearance to have been necessary so early on.

It seems a strange practice to litter arable fields with clearance cairns, although some fields were almost entirely cairn-free. For over 1000 years, however, locally grown barley seems to have been the dominant food, implying that the areas between the cairns were indeed for arable crops. Sheep became more important as time went on, and by the time the third house was in use, sheep dominated the economy. An

9 Field system, Scord of Brouster. (Alasdair Whittle)

outer field system beyond the nucleus of six fields contained few clearance cairns and was not cleared of woodland until the period of the second house.

Regular use of the fields would necessitate regular manuring. The houses were swept out frequently and the sweepings, including the ash from the fire, were dumped on to a midden outside. At intervals this was spread on to the fields. Seaweed would also have helped to keep the soil fertile.

The field walls were initially discontinuous and may have been built to demarcate plots rather than to serve as barriers. It is possible that the livestock were hobbled, tethered or herded. On the other hand, apparent breaks in the wall might have been filled with wooden hurdles or have had stone removed from them

at a later date. Wide, low walls may have supported a fence or stock-proof construction. In places, walling may still exist buried beneath the peat. Even well-constructed walls can tumble to a confusing jumble of stone with the passing of centuries; however, the irregularity of the walls would serve to strengthen them, making them more wind-resistant than straight ones.

Different types of fields are found on steeper hillsides. Agriculture carried out on a slope would cause the soil to move slowly downhill resulting in lynchets, a deep accumulation of soil against a wall, rise or other obstacle. Lynchets would take time to form – in more recent times crofters used to collect the soil from the bottom of the slope and return it to the top in order to keep the land productive.

The prehistoric settlements with houses and field walls which are visible today are often situated in fairly exposed locations between the 30 and 60m (100–200ft) contours, as at the Scord of Brouster, Sumburgh Head and Ferny Cup (Fair Isle). In each case there are no traces of houses lower down the slopes. It is probable that the remains of settlements and fields on the lower ground have been destroyed, either when the land was cleared for later agricultural developments or because the stone could be reused.

In contrast to the houses at the Scord of Brouster, some prehistoric houses such as the house at Catpund are found in the middle of an enclosure but with no other fields around them, and may be found considerably higher into the hills than the field systems. The Ordnance Survey maps record these sites as 'homesteads'. The enclosure may have served a similar function to the infields; alternatively, it may have been used to impound stock. At Catpund excavation both within the enclosure and across

its wall was uninformative. The land inside the enclosure was relatively flat, but one corner of the floor of the house had to be built up in order to make the floor level.

Ard marks

The earliest farmers brought barley to Shetland, as well as sheep and cattle. Oats were introduced later, as were pigs. The farmers had wood, bone and stone which they could fashion into tools to help them, and the ard, or prehistoric plough, was introduced very early and would have been the most efficient way of breaking new ground. Ard ploughing would seem to have been standard practice Shetland-wide; a practice which endured for around three millennia.

The ard comprised a long thin sandstone bar attached to a wooden framework and would have been pulled through the ground in order to rip a furrow (**10**). The stone ard point was usually oval or round in cross-section and

10 Remains of wooden frame of an ard found in the peat on Virdi Field. (Shetland Museum)

11 Ard ploughing in the South Mainland.
(Joanna Richards)

unbroken ards were on average 20–50cm (8–20in) long. The stone was flaked and chipped into the required shape, but would have become smooth through use. Sometimes the bars were double-ended; others were used on one side and then rotated through 180° when they became worn. In some cases, the uneven wear suggests that the ard point entered the ground at an angle.

Ards were pulled by female cattle (11). Areas taken into cultivation were fairly small and the farms were not large enough to support animals exclusively for ploughing; therefore the same cows were used for milking. Arthritis showed in the bones of cows found in Orkney, demonstrating their use as draught animals. A house excavated at Sumburgh had ard marks which ran so close to it that it seems likely that the ploughs were sometimes pulled by the farmers.

Ard ploughing broke up the ground surface but did not turn the soil over. Its effectiveness was increased by ploughing the ground in criss-cross fashion. The bottoms of the furrows may still survive as dark marks, known as 'ard marks', in the subsoil. Ard marks have been found during several excavations in Shetland, in each case associated with early fields (colour plate 1). Broken ard points are frequently found throughout the islands. At Kebister, near Lerwick, some of the ard marks ended in a broken ard point where the ard had struck against a stone in the ground and smashed.

Major boundaries

The countryside was divided by substantial boundary dykes which run for long distances, indicating that the land had been divided up extensively. These dykes are relatively straight and are sometimes aligned on hilltops or burial cairns. In some places, these dykes were built of stone. Lengths of stone dyke protrude through the peat at locations all over Shetland; one of the best areas to see them is in the West Side.

In other places 'fealie' dykes were built using turf (or feals), sometimes on a base of stone. Fealie dykes would need more regular repair and attention than stone ones. These fealie dykes could be broad at the base, and in later times were surmounted by fences or stakes to make them stock-proof. Some of the more complete examples survived due to their reuse as township or hill-land (scattald) boundaries, for example, the Funzie Girt Dyke in Fetlar. These major dykes were probably always territorial boundaries. In Fair Isle a major dyke divides the hill land (scattald) from the town-lands, but this may have been because the dyke formed a useful boundary in approximately the right position.

In the main, Shetland's hills are divided vertically as well as horizontally, as occurred at Funzie Girt in Fetlar (**12**), areas of the West Side, and Gletness in Nesting. Similar land divisions elsewhere in Britain have been ascribed tentatively to the Bronze Age, but in Shetland some of them seem to pre-date Neolithic field systems, which respect the major dykes and do not cross them. Some of the dykes even appear to predate burial cairns.

The division of even small areas of Shetland implies a high level of territorial organization as well as sufficiently large numbers of people to warrant dividing up the countryside. It suggests that there may have been a hierarchy within the society almost as soon as farmers began to settle in Shetland. Noel Fojut has suggested that there were as many as 10,000 people living in Neolithic Shetland.

12 Funzie Girt dyke. (RCAHMS)

The impact of farming

Shetland's light covering of woodland had a stabilizing effect on the land. Shetland has a naturally wet climate which would tend to wash (or leach) minerals down through the soil as well as across the surface, resulting in the soils losing their nutrients. Tree roots help to counteract these effects; by penetrating deeply they absorb nutrients which have been washed down to the lower soil horizons. The minerals are drawn up into the tree, then returned each autumn as leaf litter, so replenishing the soil. If minerals were lost faster than they could be replaced the woodland could die, either temporarily or permanently, of natural causes.

As the trees in Shetland were cut down, so iron and manganese were washed down into the soil to a level which the roots of herbaceous plants and cereals could not reach. The metals thus deposited created a solid band (an 'iron pan') which even deep-rooted plants were unable to penetrate. The iron pan also acted as a damp course, causing the soil to become waterlogged. On uncultivated hill land the surface of an impoverished soil was colonized by heathers and the soluble products of heather litter in turn accelerated the leaching. Sphagnum then began to grow on the waterlogged soil, causing it to become anaerobic (lacking in oxygen), with no worms or organisms able to live in it to break up the dead sphagnum. Dead vegetation then became compressed by the next generation of plant material which grew through it. As a result blanket peat began to form in damp hollows, and then gradually spread down the hills.

Cereal crops do not have the same long roots as trees, and are cut down before they can return nutrients to the soil. Manuring the soil and digging it over was – and is – necessary to keep the soil fertile. The Neolithic cultivation at the Scord of Brouster actually seems to have prevented the peat encroaching on to the fields for about 400 years. The transition to pasture at Brouster, however, may have had less to do with the growth of peat and more to do with the increasing stoniness of the fields. Cultivation increases the percentage of stones vis-à-vis earth in a soil, and, unless the soil is replenished, it will eventually become unworkable. Soils which were cultivated before Neolithic cairns, houses or walls were built on them tend to be deeper and richer than the acidic soils around them, which were worked for longer periods. This lends weight to the theory that the soils were worked until they became exhausted.

In spite of the worsening climate during the Bronze Age and Early Iron Age, sometimes arable activity was too important to abandon on the grounds of soil deterioration. In other cases, the original land was infertile and occasionally soils known as 'plaggen' soils were created artificially. This was done by cutting grassy turves from unenclosed areas and impregnating them with animal manures, waste, burnt ash and small amounts of seaweed, in order to maintain and improve the productivity of the soil. The soils are only a few hectares in extent and survive up to 0.75m (30in) deep. Ian Simpson has identified 'plaggen' soils in South Nesting, in Fair Isle and at Old Scatness. At Scatness these soils were cultivated using an ard, but at the Burn of Furse in Fair Isle spade cultivation created a ridge and furrow effect on the surface. The Shetland plaggen soils are some of the earliest created soils in north-west Europe.

Houses

There are currently 180 prehistoric house sites recorded in Shetland's Sites and Monuments Record (13). They were first recognized as being a group by Charles Calder, who recorded seventy-four during the 1950s; this number has been, and is still being, added to by archaeologists and amateurs alike. Inevitably, all the sites identified by observation alone are constructed of stone. Excavations at the Scord of Brouster and at Sumburgh (Runway) uncovered earlier timber structures under stone houses on both sites, and at Kebister there was a sub-rectangular timber building associated

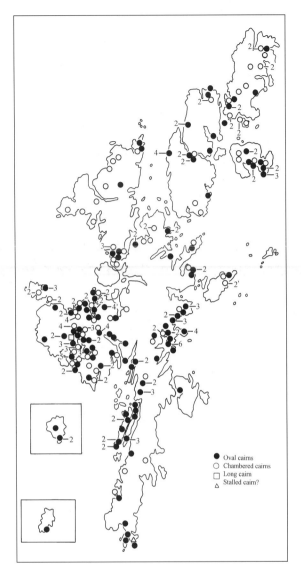

13 Prehistoric houses and cairns. (Anna Purdy)

Oval cairns
Chambered cairns
Long cairn
Stalled cairn?

the same shape as the chambered tombs and with a central entrance through the heel-shaped façade. Reasonable as this theory would appear to be, a study of the artefacts, radiocarbon dating and examination of the buildings themselves reveals a far more complex picture.

All the prehistoric stone houses were essentially oval in shape, with a single entrance at the narrower end (**14**), often protected by a porch or, later, a courtyard. Their low stone walls varied from 1 to 5m (3 to 16ft) thick, and were constructed from rubble which was faced on the inside and often on the outside as well. Inside, the majority of the houses had alcoves around the walls, either set into the walls themselves or formed by building piers which projected into the central space. The floors of the alcoves were often paved, usually higher than the central area, and bounded by a stone sill. The projecting ends of the alcoves were usually faced with a massive upright stone ('orthostat'), which in some cases may have carried masonry which helped to support the roof. The central area usually contained a hearth, although sometimes the fire was in an alcove instead.

The houses probably had low, pitched turf and heather roofs which rested on a wooden, or possibly whalebone, framework interlaced with ropes of heather or straw. Sometimes the turf was overlaid with straw, held in place by further ropes weighted down with stones tied on to their ends. The roof rested on the wall core and was given additional support by timber posts and perhaps the stone piers. This method of roof construction continued in use until the beginning of this century, and is perfectly waterproof. Inside, tools may have been stored within the rafters. This would explain why a scatter of tools is often found lying on the floor of an abandoned house; they fell down when the roof collapsed. The house would have been dark and smoky inside, with little light apart from that from the fire. As a result, archaeologists usually argue that most daily activities took place outside the house.

with a Bronze Age cooking site. These buildings may be representative of a whole group of timber prehistoric houses which leave no remains which are visible on the surface and so are only ever discovered by chance. The earliest radiocarbon-dated house in Shetland is at the Scord of Brouster, where the earliest stone house was built around 3250 BC, overlaying a wooden one.

Charles Calder attributed all the stone houses to the Neolithic period on the basis that the group includes heel-shaped houses, which were

14 A Bronze Age house site at Clickhimin. (Historic
Scotland)

Outside the entrance of the Sumburgh
(Runway) house, for example, there were raised
platforms where quartz was knapped and
coarse stone tools worked: supporting evidence
for a warmer climate than that of today.

Tools for daily living

The early settlers had access to a wide range of
natural materials which they used to create
tools, clothes and implements, most of which
do not survive. The sandy soil at Jarlshof did,
however, allow bone to survive, and bone awls,
pins and a 'plaque' of uncertain function were
all found amongst the earliest Bronze Age levels
(**15**). All the house sites excavated in Shetland
have produced large quantities of stone tools,
most of which were made from easily
obtainable local stone. Some stones were used

as they were; any suitably sized stone could be
used as a hammer stone, and a split beach
pebble was all that was required to use as a
grain rubber. The three house sites at the Scord
of Brouster produced 545 'rough stone'
implements (**16**), most of which were made
from sandstone, which is local to the West Side.
The tools were fashioned by chipping off large
flakes. The number of sandstone flakes found
in the two oval houses suggests that tools were
being made inside both buildings. Large
numbers of the tools had been broken either in
use or during manufacture.

In the South Mainland numbers of tools are
made from slate, which splits easily to form
cutting and chopping implements. Slate knives,
hand-sized flat slabs and a 'handled chopper'
were found in the earliest levels at Jarlshof. A
prehistoric house and field system lie beneath
the ridge which runs between Compass Head
and Sumburgh Head (**17**). Just above the field

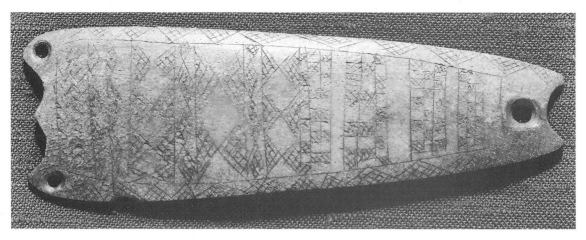

15 Decorated bone 'plaque' from the early Bronze Age levels at Jarlshof (12cm (5in) long). (National Museums of Scotland)

16 Rough stone tools from Jarlshof. (Historic Scotland)

17 A farming settlement near Sumburgh Head. (Joanna Richards)

system there is a densely packed area of shallow quarry pits and scoops, which follows an outcrop of slate. These quarries may well have been the source of many of the slate tools found in the South Mainland.

There is also a wide range of stone tools of uncertain function. These include axe-shaped tools, and flat rectangular-sectioned tools, which may have been used in the preparation of clay or for peat cutting. Tools with angled faces may have been coarse tools for cleaning skins or working leather. Stone discs are described as pot lids. Some of the more amorphous tools may have been attached to wood or bone handles and used as farm tools. Mattocks and hoes would have been required in addition to ards to work the land.

In contrast, handled clubs were fashioned with more care (**18**). The clubs were made of sandstone, but they represent a stage which is midway between the rough stone tools and the polished stone axes and mace heads of highly polished fine-grained stone. The stone was chipped into shape, then smoothed down. In several cases, the clubs were decorated with incised bands. These top-of-the-range 'rough tools' were probably Bronze Age and demonstrate the high degree of skill which the Shetlanders clearly possessed.

Querns, used for grinding grain, were often made from blocks of sandstone. They may have been fairly flat-topped when they were first used, but constant grinding would make the 'dish' in the top deeper and wider. Grain ground with a hand quern would have been rather gritty, and would have worn down people's teeth quite dramatically.

There was no natural flint with which to make blades; quartz was the closest material indigenous to Shetland. Quartz was much harder to work as it was often flawed, which caused tools to break during manufacture. Quartz scrapers and knives are hard to identify, as unworked quartz breaks naturally to a fairly sharp edge, but the delicate leaf-shaped arrowheads are unmistakable (**19**).

18 Stone club from Caldbeck, Unst. (Shetland Museum)

Pottery

The clay for making pots was found in pockets and may never have been of a very high quality. As the Neolithic Shetlanders did not have access to the potter's wheel, the majority of pots were made by coiling 'worms' of clay around a flat base and then smoothing them down to create a flat surface. Sometimes the pot was decorated before it was fired. Grits were added to the clay (described as 'tempering') in order to prevent the pot from shattering when it was fired. Steatite, known to

19 Worked quartz. Top arrowhead is barbed and tanged. (Shetland Museum)

the Neolithic settlers as a soft, workable stone, was commonly used as tempering because it was so easy to crush.

Some of the pottery found on Shetland sites resembles Orcadian pottery; three bowls found in the cist burial at Sumburgh were plain with rounded bases, although they lacked the distinctive Orcadian Unstan Ware hatched decoration. It would appear that the incoming

33

Neolithic Shetlanders were quick to develop their own style of pottery.

A time and shape?

Radiocarbon dates are now available for several house sites in Shetland; it is therefore possible to examine the evidence from the excavated sites to try to discern a sequence in the shapes of houses (**20**).

In the series of three stone houses at the Scord of Brouster the earliest, constructed about 3250 BC, was oval, with a kidney-shaped interior which was essentially an open space. The second house, constructed in about 2750 BC, appears to

have been used for around 1000 years (**21**). It was a well-built oval house with two recesses edged with sills on each long side and two less prominent recesses at the far end. The inner face of the wall was lined with flat stones, to a height of about 0.5m (20in); the wall was essentially a dump wall of earth, stone of various sizes (although with larger stones at the base) and midden material, but there was no well-defined outer face. The third building, constructed around 1750 BC, was another oval house with five recesses. Both the internal and external edges of the recesses were carefully faced, and one of the orthostats stood 1.05m (3ft 6in) high, indicating that the walls must have been of at least a similar height. A second oval structure adjacent to the house had no internal divisions and was probably an outhouse or workshop.

20 Prehistoric house sites which evolved during the Neolithic/Bronze Age in Shetland (after Calder, Hamilton, Downes). (Val Turner)

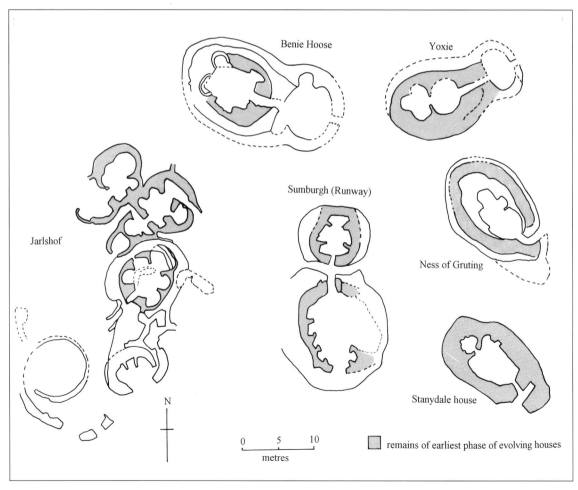

21 Second stone house to be built at the Scord of Brouster.
(Alasdair Whittle)

At the Scord of Brouster each house had an
extremely long life-span but did not undergo
major structural changes. Other houses had a
more varied existence. The Benie Hoose in
Whalsay went through three building phases.
Initially, it was built as an oval house, with an
irregular interior containing two recesses and a
series of drains. The wall was a dump of earth
and stones which was faced. In time, the outside
structure was adapted to give the house a heel-
shaped exterior which lengthened the entrance,
and the inside was modified with additional
recesses. The heel-shaped front was faced with
large boulders. Midden material, especially peat-
ash, which built up around the house while it

was in use, was incorporated within the dump
walls. A third cladding changed the shape of the
house yet again, this time to a figure-of-eight or
courtyard house. The forecourt was roughly
circular inside, retaining the heel-shaped face as
its back wall. The enclosed space may have
continued to serve some of the functions of the
previous open-air space in front of the heel-
shaped façade.

A short distance from the Benie Hoose, Yoxie
was constructed as an oval house with two
distinctive chambers: a circular cell and an inner
trefoil-shaped cell. When the wall was
thickened, a forecourt was added, creating a
figure-of-eight-shaped house. Whether or not
there was an intermediate heel-shaped stage is
unclear; there was no trace of a wall-face
relating to such a stage but, like the Benie

Hoose, Yoxie has a heel-shaped back to the forecourt. One of the structures excavated at Kebister, near Lerwick, had a heel-shaped façade. It was the second of a series of buildings, the earliest being timber and the later buildings being firmly dated to the Iron Age. Although the building was very fragmentary, the façade was clear and the structure has been dated tentatively to the Late Bronze Age.

When Charles Calder and Whalsay-born teacher John Stewart excavated the Benie Hoose, Yoxie and also the Ness of Gruting, they assumed that the multiple wall-faces were all part of the primary construction. It is a tribute to the high standard of the work of these excavators that archaeologists can now reassess the site by re-examining the original records.

At the Ness of Gruting there were two identifiable building phases: both oval houses. Like the Whalsay houses, the second building phase incorporated midden material, including a

cache of 12.7kg (28lb) of carbonized barley and an adjacent quern stone which lay up against the earlier wall (**22**). The grain was radiocarbon dated to around 2000 BC. It may have been a religious offering for the future prosperity of the house, or perhaps it was thrown out on to the midden around the house and so incorporated into the extension more or less by accident. There are precedents for building houses into midden material in Scotland: at Skara Brae in Orkney seven of the eight houses are built into midden, although, unlike the Shetland houses, they are not actually constructed using midden material. Interestingly, the eighth Skara Brae house, which stands apart from the village, is built in a similar style to the Shetland houses.

Dumping midden material around the house would have served to cut down draughts and so keep the inside warmer. An outer wall-face may have revetted the midden as well as helping to contain it within a restricted area, rather than leaving it to spread over a wider area or blow about. In widening the walls there was no necessity to alter the roof shape or area; the

22 Ness of Gruting. Carbonized barley from the house wall. (RCAHMS)

additional wall-cores were loosely packed, and run-off from the roof would have drained through them freely. The porch wall at the Ness of Gruting was thickened when it was buttressed, and at a later stage field-clearance stones were thrown up against the porch. The Scord of Brouster houses were also used as convenient clearance cairns. Thickening the walls and changing their shape may have been, at least in part, a pragmatic response to waste disposal and heating! Even so, the heel shape of the façades was a consistent feature, the result of deliberate planning.

The houses at Jarlshof and Clickhimin were dated by their excavators on the basis of the finds. At Jarlshof there are four recessed oval houses, one of which contains souterrains (**23**) (see Chapter 5). By the time that bronze was worked in this house, it had already had a long life. It was then turned into a courtyard house, which was in turn superseded by an open round house with far thinner walls. The use of Iron Age technology began during the round-house

23 This oval recessed house at Jarlshof was converted into the northern half of a courtyard house late in the Bronze Age. There is a souterrain in the centre of the house which curves around the hearth. A second, external, souterrain can be entered by visitors via the wooden hatch (extreme right). (Historic Scotland)

period. Clickhimin started life in the Bronze Age as a village of open oval houses. Recessed oval houses were included at a later date, and a thin-walled round house was added around the beginning of the Iron Age.

The house which now lies beneath Sumburgh Airport's east–west runway was excavated when the runway was extended in the early 1970s, and has proved to be slightly unusual in the sequence of Shetland houses (see **20**). Unlike most of the other excavated house sites, the Sumburgh (Runway) house was on low-lying land, and today stands only 4m (13ft) above sea level. The area was, and still is, subject to frequent sand blow which periodically covered the fields and houses and, as at Jarlshof, it may have been this sand which preserved the site from later stone robbing. The northern section of the stone house overlies the remains of a timber building which may have been built as much as 800 years earlier. In spite of the ever-present dangers of the sand, people lived in the area fairly continuously. Although there was a break in the occupation between the two houses, it is likely that the area was never completely abandoned. It is more probable that the focus of settlement shifted slightly. As the rescue excavation concentrated on the house site, any shift in settlement would not have been located.

The first stone house at Sumburgh (Runway) took the form of an oval house which has been interpreted as having a trefoil chamber and an outer round chamber like that at Yoxie. The chambers are ill-defined, however, and it is possible that the house may originally have been built as a recessed house with five alcoves. The house excavated near Stanydale 'temple' is recessed but had an inner chamber at the far end; an inner chamber at The Gairdie looks more like an enlarged recess; perhaps end recesses were devolved from inner chambers – or *vice versa*. In any event, the courtyard was later added to the south of the Sumburgh (Runway) house, more than doubling the space inside. The surrounding wall was thickened with midden material, rubble and earth and was revetted periodically.

The entrance to the Sumburgh (Runway) house was in the southern end of the courtyard, having the main living space right at the back of the house, as at the Benie Hoose and Yoxie. The courtyard contained a large central hearth, with a paved area to the west. A cluster of artefacts in the area suggested that this was where tools and clothes were made and repaired and food was cooked. Tether posts and heart-shaped stone pieces, found in the southern end of the courtyard, were probably part of animal tethers, indicating that cattle were housed there, albeit seasonally. The northern area of the house was used far less. The hearth and tank (a stone slab-lined box) had gone out of use and was perhaps now reserved for sleeping.

Soon after 1000 BC, the whole house was remodelled. The entrance at the south end of the courtyard was sealed up and a cross-passage inserted between the north and south areas, giving access to people approaching the house from the east and west. It was at this stage that working surfaces were created on platforms outside the entrances, and the focus of settlement shifted back into the northern area. The hearth in the southern courtyard was paved over and hearths were inserted into all but one of the bays in the northern chamber. Cooking was now carried out in the northern segment, whilst the southern segment was used primarily for storage. Livestock still seem to have been kept in the southern half, but it must have been difficult to manoeuvre them through the narrow passage.

Strangely, when the new east–west corridor was built, it was constructed with a curve which gave the courtyard area a heel-shaped façade. The builders accentuated the façade by lining it with orthostats. In other excavated prehistoric houses, the heel shape predates the building of a courtyard and the façade was constructed in front of the principal living area. When the courtyard was added the original façade usually became the back wall, and so the area in front of it could continue to be used for ceremony even though it ceased to be impressive from a distance. The façade of the Sumburgh (Runway) house is effectively on the wrong half. It is unlikely ever to have been used for ceremonial purposes because it formed one side of a corridor and space was very limited. It may have served to make the entrance to the southern section appear more grand, although it could never have been viewed from any distance. Nevertheless the heel shape, which was by this time as much as 3000 years old, must still have had significance for Shetlanders living at the end of the Bronze Age.

Jane Downes's analysis of the Sumburgh (Runway) house is one of the most detailed studies made of an excavated prehistoric oval house in Shetland. It presents a very complex picture of a living, evolving family who adjusted their surroundings to suit their changing needs and individual circumstances, just as we would today. It is perhaps the closest we can get in attempting to establish what people thought and what their priorities were.

Not all houses underwent such extensive changes or were replaced *in situ*. Some houses had a shorter life-span, perhaps because they were situated on poorer land.

When all the information is taken together, a pattern begins to emerge. The earliest prehistoric houses seem to have been built in wood, a practice which could have continued whenever new areas of woodland were opened up for farming. Next to be built were oval houses with fairly open living areas. These were followed in turn by recessed oval houses, heel-shaped houses, courtyard houses encased in a figure-of-eight surrounding wall, and finally thin-walled, open round houses which started to

be built shortly before the commencement of the Iron Age (**24**).

The chronological span for each house type is broad. The earliest oval open houses, represented at the Scord of Brouster and Mavis Grind, span a period of more than 1000 years. Oval recessed houses such as the second Scord of Brouster house overlap this period. This house was constructed around 2750 BC and may have been lived in for 1000 years. The Wiltrow house (see Chapter 5), on the other hand, may not have been built until around the beginning of the Iron Age, around 800 BC. Heel-shaped houses do not seem to have had an early Neolithic date; where dating evidence does exist, at Sumburgh (Runway) and at Kebister, they seem to have been built late in the Neolithic period and during the Bronze Age. Curiously then, the heel-shaped houses appear to have been built as much as

24 Diagram demonstrating the changes in house shape, together with dates where these are known (LBA = Late Bronze Age; EIA = Early Iron Age). (Val Turner)

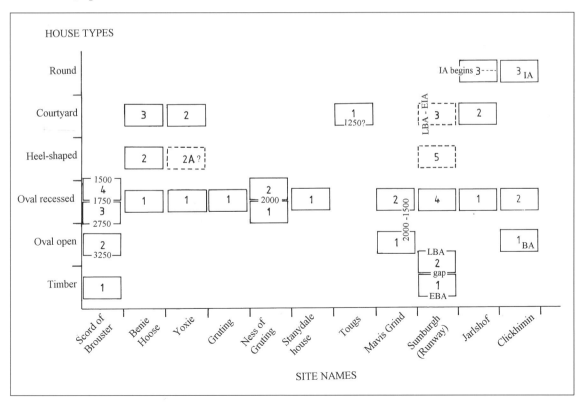

1000 years later than the heel-shaped burial cairns (see Chapter 4).

The information which archaeologists find tends to be biased towards the houses on the slightly higher, marginal land; land that would have been abandoned once the climate deteriorated and the soil became exhausted or covered in peat. These sites are likely to be those which were occupied well into the Bronze Age, since which time the hill land has been occupied less intensively. House sites on more fertile land will be more difficult to find unless, as at Sumburgh (Runway) and at Jarlshof, they have been protected by natural causes such as sand blow; more commonly later settlement will have destroyed the earlier evidence. Until such time as further excavation and radio-carbon dating have tested this, a sequence of fashions in building stone houses which can be traced over a period of almost 3000 years, it would be premature to ascribe precise dates to each category.

4
Death and ritual

By analogy with mainland Scotland, Neolithic burial cairns are thought to predate any of the house or field systems which have been excavated so far. The implication is that the cairn builders lived in houses of timber or other perishable materials which are less easy to identify than stone.

Burials in boxes

The earliest dated burial in Shetland is an unusually large cist burial (25), found when the present control tower was built at Sumburgh Airport in 1977. Radiocarbon dating placed it between 3235 and 3135 BC. The cist comprised a pit, lined with boulders set on edge. It was built on compact sand and may originally have been covered by a mound. The cist contained the bones of at least eighteen individuals: ten adults, four juveniles and four new-born infants. Although it was not possible to determine the sex of each individual, the burial included both males and females, one of whom was over 40 years old. The remains were disarticulated: they were already reduced to bones when they were placed in the cist. The bodies had either been buried and exhumed before being moved into the cist, or left out in the open air until sufficiently decomposed. The cist burial was accompanied by three plain bowls, five stone beads, stone tools and a polished stone adze, all of which had been made locally.

A cist burial containing so many bodies is almost unique in Scotland, but the Sumburgh burial might be one of several such burials contemporary with the chambered cairns which are more common. Assuming that the Shetland chambered cairns were built at the same time as those in the rest of Scotland, they may be as early as 4000 BC, and have continued in use until about 2500 BC.

Burials on hilltops

Chambered cairns were often built in prominent locations, on hilltops or on knolls and rises. The cairn situated on the summit of Ronas Hill (the highest hill in Shetland) is, at 450m (1475ft), the highest chambered cairn in Scotland.

Burying the dead in prominent places is common throughout the pagan world. It may have been important to the living to be constantly reminded of their ancestors, or perhaps the ancestors wanted to watch over their community. Neolithic Shetlanders were constantly at the mercy of the weather: being close to the sky, or on the skyline, may have been important to them.

In contrast, the cairn at Islesburgh is close to the high-water mark. Most of the cairns are found close to land which could be cultivated and support a population. The lower-lying cairns are usually found in very fertile areas. Ronas Hill and the Beorgs of Uyea are notable exceptions, but are close to the axe factory.

None of the cairns is very large: Vementry is one of the biggest, with a chamber about 2m (6ft) high (**colour plate 2**). At the Beorgs of Uyea the

25 Finds from the Sumburgh cist. (Shetland Museum)

passage and chamber are virtually subterranean. The cairns may never have been much larger than they are today and their tops may have been fairly flat, level with the roof of the chamber.

The majority of Shetland's chambered cairns are described as heel-shaped. Apart from one cairn found in Caithness, heel-shaped cairns are unique to Shetland. Like the houses previously discussed, heel-shaped cairns are essentially oval, constructed with coursed masonry or faced with orthostats, with a concave façade at one end. The façade is usually the best-built part of the cairn. Invariably there was either an orthostat or a conveniently situated rock outcrop at each end of the façade.

Façades vary from cairn to cairn. The 'Giant's Grave' in Northmavine has such a pronounced

face that it resembles the horns found on other Scottish chambered cairns. By contrast, the northern cairn on Vord Hill in Fetlar has an almost flat façade. In some cases, the façade seems to have been added after the cairn had gone out of use, so blocking the entrance passage.

Some façades have entrances in the centre, and most of the entrances face between south and east. The entrance passage leads to a cruciform or rectangular central chamber. The roof of the chambers and passage was normally covered with large slabs. Several cairns have a lot of stone on the forecourt in front of the façade. At some the stone appears to have been placed there deliberately and even revetted; at others, such as Vementry, it is clear that the stone has fallen from the cairn.

Two chambered cairns (Scord of Scalloway and South Nesting Hall) have been excavated recently. The cairn at the Scord of Scalloway was on the top of a hill, and disclosed no finds other than a piece of pumice. The heel-shaped cairn near South Nesting Hall was situated below the shoulder of a low rise. The cairn had been disturbed when it was incorporated into a field boundary and cultivation lynchet at some time before the Iron Age. It was, however, reused in the Bronze Age, and tiny fragments of cremated bone and pottery, possibly part of a cremation vessel, were found.

An Orcadian connection?

Not all the chambered cairns were heel-shaped (26); a few appear to have been round and others, such as the March Cairn in the North Mainland, were clearly square. In addition, there are three cairns, Trolligerts and Dale in the West Side and Sumburgh Head, which may have been built in the style of Orcadian cairns, i.e. divided into compartments, formed by slabs on end. The long cairns at Trolligerts and Dale are very disturbed, and it is difficult to be certain whether they were stalled. Excavation at the other, on Sumburgh Head, should reveal whether this site was a Bookan-style cairn, with a sub-circular series of compartments divided by slabs on edge. With the exception of Fair Isle, this site could hardly have been found closer to Orkney. There are very few known Neolithic

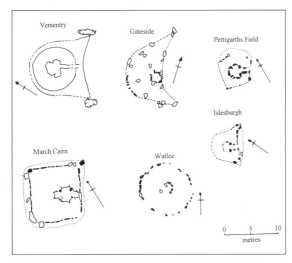

26 Plans of chambered cairns. (Val Turner)

links between Orkney and Shetland, house 8 at Skara Brae being almost the only known exception. Yet some Orcadians must have travelled to Shetland, even if the bulk of incomers were from mainland Scotland. Sumburgh Head would be a logical place at which to find a link.

Cairns without chambers

There are a few cairns which do not seem to have had central chambers; in some cases excavation might reveal a burial chamber, while in others there were cists instead. The cairn at Muckle Heog East, in the island of Unst, was excavated during the last century. Bones were discovered in two cists, one of which contained a skull together with fragments of pottery and steatite vessels, similar to Bronze Age vessels found both at Jarlshof and in a two-storey cist at Asta, Tingwall. On the assumption that the cists were part of the original use of the cairn, this suggests that the cairn was built at the time when burial practices were beginning to move away from chambered cairns towards other forms of burial.

The partially excavated kerb cairn at the Scord of Brouster contained no evidence of any burial chamber. It began as a small circular cairn to which a well-defined kerb of large stones was added later. The cairn was covered with smaller stones. The edge differentiates the cairn from the clearance cairns around it, but its use for burial remains unproven.

Last rites

The heel-shaped façade, common to the majority of the Shetland chambered cairns, probably had a ritual purpose. The forecourt in front of the façade may have been the area where ceremonies took place or last rites were administered. As some façades were not completed until the burial chamber was sealed, they may have been intended to indicate the importance of the ancestors or their associated living relatives. The façade would make the cairn look impressive to anyone approaching, and make it more visible at a distance. This could explain why the cairn at Vementry was built close to a fairly steep drop; it would have added to the impressiveness of the cairn.

The bodies may have been laid out in front of the cairn for a period, and only moved into the cairn once they had reduced to bones. If a body was put into the cairn when the person was recently dead, many of the cairns would only have been large enough to hold one body. If, as in Orcadian stalled cairns, parts of many individuals were buried together, the Shetland cairns would have been able to hold many more of the ancestors. In Orkney parts of as many as 160 bodies have been found buried together. These bodies were not complete; sometimes bones were neatly stacked in piles, with long bones in one area and skulls in another.

The Shetland Neolithic dead were not well-provisioned for the after-life. The finds from the cairns seem to have been incidental. The square March Cairn contained a quartz flake and two tiny stone discs, but these were found well above the floor level of the burial chamber. Sherds of pottery from Pettigarth's Field in Whalsay seem to have been mixed with the covering stone, and a possible late Neolithic (beaker) sherd from Hestingsetter, on the West Side, was lost. The pumice from the Scord of Scalloway was almost certainly incidental.

Building a cairn would require the effort of a community of people, and the territorial dykes show that the Neolithic peoples were accustomed to such co-operative ventures. Not everyone could have been buried in the chambered cairns – there are nowhere near enough! We do not know how people were selected for burial in a cairn; perhaps they were the community leaders or important people. Nor do we have any idea of what happened to the rest of the population. Even if more cairns and more cists like the Sumburgh cist are found, there would still be large numbers of people unaccounted for: people who were either buried in the ground without a stone memorial, or perhaps buried at sea. In either case, it is unlikely that we will ever find any evidence.

Indeed, bones rarely survive in the Shetland cairns as the covering material was loose stone which would not help preservation. As far as we know, the bones were laid straight on to the ground, which was either bare rock or a thin covering of soil. The chambered tombs look set to hold on to many of their secrets.

A Neolithic temple?

The site at Stanydale, West Mainland, is situated in the centre of a bowl of flat land surrounded by hills, many of which have cairns on their summits. Unusually for Shetland, it is not possible to glimpse the sea, or a loch, in any direction from the site. Today the area is wet and boggy, but in Neolithic times it contained several farms. The 'temple' site is surrounded by the remains of stone dykes, of which some may be territorial dykes and others field boundaries (**27**). There are several house sites close by. One of these which has been excavated was oval with a porch at one end, and may have been earlier than the 'temple'.

Charles Calder excavated Stanydale in the 1950s. It was double the size of any prehistoric house, measuring 12 by 7m (39 by 22ft) inside; the walls were 4–5m (12–17ft) thick, constructed of massive blocks of stone, some of which stood on end. The largest and best stones were reserved for the inside face and were as much as 1.25m (3ft 10in) tall. The building is Shetland's only truly megalithic (large stone) monument.

Like the burial cairns, Stanydale is heel-shaped, but the pottery found in it dates it to around the end of the Neolithic period (2500–2000 BC), by which time the period of cairn building was essentially over. The building may have been in use for over 1000 years, as it also contained pottery fragments which appear to date from the broch period. As we have seen, a number of houses were converted to heel shapes at around the time that Stanydale was built. The stone-faced, heel-shaped façade, also found on the tombs, was clearly important.

Charles Calder described Stanydale as a 'temple' because it resembled the shape, but not

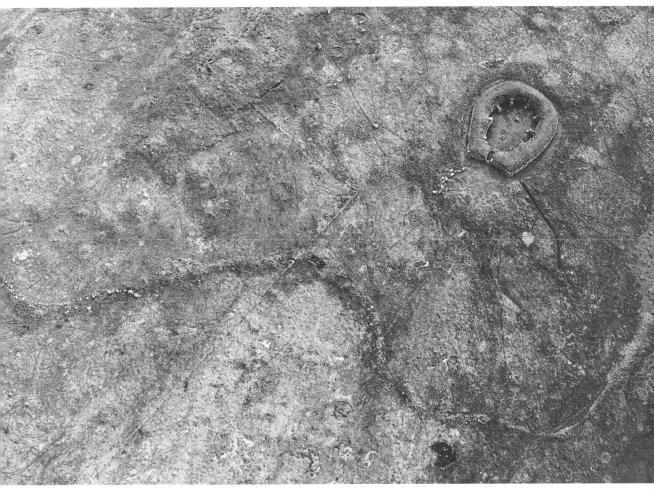

27 Stanydale. Field system and 'temple'. (Historic Scotland)

the construction, of buildings known to be Neolithic temples in Malta. The finds from the Maltese buildings included female figurines, but there have been no such finds from Stanydale, or indeed anywhere else in Shetland. It seems improbable that the Shetlanders followed the same religion as the Maltese.

Like many of the house sites, Stanydale has six recesses, each roughly 2.6m (8ft) long, set approximately 1.25m (4ft) into the thick internal wall. They are far bigger than the usual sleeping and workshop alcoves. Each dividing partition ends in an orthostat which continues the line of the wall-face. There was no central hearth in the building, but the ashy remains of several small hearths were found in front of the

recesses. The floor was clean, unlike the floors of ordinary houses, which are usually found covered in ash, broken pottery and other domestic rubbish. The few finds from Stanydale included two fragments of a polished stone 'Shetland knife' (see pages 49–50 below), probably a ritual object, as well as quartz cores and chips.

In the centre of the building are two large post-holes, one of which contained the carbonized stumps of two spruce posts set side by side. The larger of these had an almost complete cross-section 25cm (10in) in diameter. The pair of uprights was probably lashed together to give the structure extra stability. On the assumption that the roof was covered by turf, heather or straw, it must have been supported by a heavy timber framework which rested on the wall-head.

Fragments of spruce and pine, found lying on the floor, probably came from such a framework. Calder calculated that making the frame would require lengths of finished timber of 8m (26ft) and 6m (20ft) and that the total length of dressed timber required would be 700m (2300ft). Although there was woodland in Shetland, it would not have produced large quantities of timber of this size, added to which spruce did not grow in Neolithic Shetland or even Scotland. Jim Dixon has explored the three possible explanations for where the wood came from. Either it was native to Shetland but predated the Ice Age, or it had been deliberately imported, or it was driftwood. Calder favoured the explanation that the timber had been imported from Scandinavia. Spruce, however, did not begin to grow along the west coast of Scandinavia until the beginning of the Iron Age, by which time Stanydale had gone out of use. We can safely assume that driftwood trunks (including a high proportion of spruce) arrived in Shetland in large quantities from North America. In 1577 'great

Firre trees' were reported by a traveller as floating in the North Atlantic, and this provided the bulk of Iceland's fuel. Spruce is very light and comparatively resistant to waterlogging, and experiments with marked bottles suggest that it would only take 12–18 months to cross the Atlantic after falling into the sea. So far, spruce has been found on five excavated prehistoric sites in Shetland, and one piece from Clickhimin contains holes made by the sea worm.

Whether or not Stanydale was a real temple, its size suggests that it had a specialized use (28). Stanydale may have served the whole of Shetland, or perhaps it was only people on the West Side who desired such a building. It would have been a place where the community came together, whatever the reason. It was clearly not simply a large or important house: the lack of stone tools and the clean interior suggest an alternative use; the polished knives may have been ritual relics. Curiously, no similar buildings have been found

28 Stanydale (Joanna Richards)

29 Standing stone, Boardastubble, Unst. (RCAHMS)

in other centres of Neolithic population. Other sites may have been destroyed by later activity. Unlike many of the house sites, Stanydale did not evolve from an oval structure into a heel shape. The thick walls were constructed with large stones rather than midden material. Stanydale seems to have been built to imitate the houses (or vice-versa), but for a different purpose. The fact that the heel shape originated with the earlier tombs adds weight to the argument that Stanydale had a religious function.

Standing stones

Standing stones have probably been erected in Shetland from the time that Neolithic people first arrived until the present day, and it is often difficult (if not impossible) to date them (29). Stones were erected for a variety of reasons, only some of which were connected to beliefs. There are, however, no true stone circles in Shetland: the possible candidates have either turned out to be enclosures (for example, Wormadale, Central Mainland) or appear to be Bronze Age cairns (for example, Rounds of Tivla, Unst).

A large standing stone at Wester Skeld, 2.8m (9ft) high by 1.9m (6ft) broad, was erected close to where six Shetland knives were buried, probably to mark the spot. The pair of 'Giant's Stones' in North Roe are really two end stones, all that remains from the façade of a heel-shaped cairn. The house site at Yoxie, in Whalsay, was known as 'the Standing Stones of Yoxie' on account of the orthostats which were visible before the house was excavated.

An east–west line of three standing stones in Eshaness, also known as 'Giant's Stones', may have been part of a 'stone row', a type of ritual monument found in other parts of Neolithic Britain. Today, only two of the three stones, recorded in 1774, survive. A group of three stones next to the Old North Road in Lerwick is all that remain of a larger group. Lines of smaller stones at Lumbister, Yell, have been described as Neolithic stone rows, but are probably the remains of the rigs of a croft which was worked in the post-medieval period.

Other standing stones appear to be boundary markers. Large stones up to 3m (10ft) tall mark the limits of a territorial boundary; a discontinuous line of smaller stones, perhaps less than a metre (3ft) high, defines the edges of a field as at the Scord of

30 Mace heads: large = unprovenanced, small = from Brindister, Hillswick. (Shetland Museum)

Brouster; the latter was soon infilled as a result of field clearance.

The sea has always been fundamental to people living in Shetland, and some standing stones were erected both as navigational marks and in order to identify meads (positions at sea). Navigation marks assisted boats in approaching harbours safely and avoiding hazards below the surface; useful meads would include those for areas of good fishing. In both cases, a stone which was visible from the sea was lined up either with another stone or with a point on the horizon. Stones erected as sea markers could be of almost any date, and even excavation may not be able to fix them in time. Two standing stones at Mulla, Unst, when lined up with each other, are also in line with a noost (see Chapter 10) on the shore below.

Stones which are lying down are described as 'recumbent stones'; most of them are standing stones which have fallen over. Cup-marked stones are marked with circular depressions which were pecked into the stone, probably during the Bronze Age. They are not common in Shetland, but there are about thirty cup marks in two separate groups in Whalsay, and a third group has been discovered recently in Unst (**colour plate 3**). Cup-marked stones may resemble recumbent stones, but are usually outcrops of bedrock.

Modern standing stones are usually located beside new or improved roads. Many have dates carved on to them, but others, such as the stone next to the long cairn at Dale, could easily be mistaken for prehistoric standing stones: the stone at Dale was in fact erected in (AD) 1989!

Shetland knives

Stone axes were manufactured throughout Britain during the Neolithic period. They were made from fine-grained igneous and volcanic rocks, such as the igneous rocks in the North Mainland, and were highly polished. The polished tools would have been perfectly functional, but they seem to have been for show rather than for everyday work.

In addition to pear-shaped axes and cylindrical 'mace heads' (**30**), there was a type of tool which was unique to Shetland: the 'Shetland knife' (**colour plate 4**). The Shetland knives were flaked from the beautiful speckled and banded porphyritic felsites, a rock-type found in Britain only in Shetland at the Beorgs of Uyea. Axes and mace heads made from Shetland felsite were traded as far as northern England, and at least one axe from the Cumbrian Langdale axe factory has been found in Shetland. The knives, however, seem to have been exclusive to Shetland and were never traded further afield.

Craftsmen made the knives from slabs of rock; they then ground both the flat sides down,

in order to produce highly polished oval discs, sometimes no more than 4mm (¼in) thick and 15–20cm (6–8in) long. When the knives were first made, all the edges were sharp, but one edge was usually ground smooth, presumably to allow it to be used safely. A few of the knives were used as tools; sometimes they are found with edges which were worn, or even resharpened. The majority, however, do not seem to have been used as cutting implements; their blades are intact. They seem rather to have served a ceremonial purpose.

A 'factory' for making stone tools has been found at the Beorgs of Uyea. One of the several working areas discovered here was a rock

31 Rock shelter at the Beorgs of Uyea. (Shetland Museum)

shelter which had been roofed (**31**). The shelter covered a hollow which had been quarried into good-quality felsite, and tools had been roughed-out (chipped into a basic shape) under the cover of the shelter. Axes or knives which broke while they were being roughed-out were abandoned on site, but successful ones were taken home to be polished.

Most of the knives have been found from undated contexts, although they are associated with late Neolithic pottery. The fact that some of the Shetland stone axes bear a resemblance to early flat bronze axes suggests that stone knives were being manufactured into the Bronze Age.

Some of the knives have been discovered buried in groups in the peat. One group, from Northmavine, was found laid out in a circle; a group of nineteen knives from Stourbrough Hill, Sandness, was arranged on end, held in place between two blocks of sandstone resembling book-ends. Knives were sometimes buried in the peat a long way from any known prehistoric occupation: perhaps they were offerings to appease the peat as it began to spread.

5
Darkening skies

The period between 1800 and 600 BC is traditionally known as the 'Bronze Age', although there is little evidence for any bronze in Shetland until towards the end of this time-span. It could almost be argued that Shetland never experienced an 'Early' or 'Middle' Bronze Age.

Elsewhere in Britain, however, the introduction of bronze was associated with changes in people's life-styles (see Chapter 3). As we have already seen, in Shetland there was no alteration in house shape which could be directly attributed to a Bronze Age 'revolution', and in many ways people's domestic lives did not undergo much change. Pottery styles altered, apparently influenced by the new styles of burial, stone 'handled clubs' were probably introduced in this period and polished stone axes took the shape of bronze axes, as if in an attempt to imitate them. In mainland Britain the shape of flint arrowheads also altered; now they had a barb on either side of the tangs which were attached to shafts of wood or bone. This was not very significant in Shetland as quartz did not easily lend itself to the new style. Two new types of structure, burnt mounds and souterrains, began to be built in Shetland during this period, both of which are restricted to geographical pockets throughout the British Isles.

Storm clouds gather

Perhaps the most dramatic change to take place in Shetland between 1800 and 600 BC had nothing whatsoever to do with the appearance of bronze. From 1500 BC the climate began to deteriorate; by 500 BC it was 2°C cooler and much more stormy than previously, and the amount of precipitation had increased. In fact, the climate was very similar to that of today. Recent studies of tephra, microscopic volcanic dust, have shown that the period coincides with an eruption of Mount Hekla, in Iceland. The dust from the eruption travelled as far as Scotland and has been identified in the soils around Kebister, near Lerwick, as well as in peat which formed at the time. It is possible that the amount of volcanic dust in the atmosphere was sufficient to reduce the sunlight to such an extent that the climate was altered.

The worsening weather led to the spread of blanket bog from damp hollows and hilltops, which in turn led to the formation of peat. Farmers were forced to move down the hillside on to lower land, although that land was already populated. At the same time, sea level was rising; even a small increase would have had a dramatic effect on some of the best agricultural land. Land which was low-lying and gently sloping would have been submerged. The population was being squeezed from both above and below!

These climatic changes would have had a drastic effect on agriculture. Crops would have failed more frequently; Shetland was always fairly marginal. As harvests failed, people would have had to rely more heavily on animals, and probably on the sea (although the sea was also

becoming more treacherous). An increase in
animal husbandry put different stresses on the
land. Too many animals would have churned up
the ground, particularly if it was wet. The
overgrazing of sheep and goats would have
wiped out some species of plants and prevented
them from returning. Throughout Shetland the
species-rich grasslands of the Neolithic period
were turning into heath. Areas of heath were
managed throughout the Neolithic and Bronze
Age by muir-burn. Overburning, however,
would have led to acidification, waterlogging
and, ultimately, peat growth, as well as the
spread of heather. Meanwhile, strong salty
winds restricted the types of vegetation which
could re-establish themselves. Some plants could
now grow only in sheltered, stock-free areas
with good brown soils. Life was becoming
altogether more precarious.

Journey's end?

The most distinctive change of culture between
the Neolithic and what followed was a change
in the style of burial. The Neolithic chambered
cairns, which probably housed numbers of
bodies, were abandoned in favour of a new
burial fashion which was sweeping across
Britain: 'Beaker burials'. In these burials bodies
were generally buried singly, in cists, boxes of
stone slabs on end, constructed in a similar way
to the Neolithic multiple cist found at Sumburgh
Airport. In this style of burial, the body was
usually laid on one side with the knees drawn
up to the chest.

A cist, of two side and two end slabs, was
excavated at the end of the nineteenth century on
top of Virdi Field in the South Mainland.
Although it was the right size to have contained a
crouched burial, as is so often the case with
prehistoric burials in Shetland the cist was empty.

A group of eight cists was found buried
below ground level when a mound at Wester
Quarff, near Lerwick, was removed in 1900.
The corners of each cist were jointed with clay.
One cist contained part of a steatite urn and a
skull; another contained ashes.

The people buried in cists seem to have been
sent to the after-life accompanied by a drink,
and perhaps, some food. This may have been
intended to be eaten during the journey, or it
may have been an offering for a gate-keeper or a
god who waited at the other end. The drink was
put into distinctive highly decorated, tall, thin-
walled pottery vessels which archaeologists have
called 'beakers'. Analysis of the residues in some
of the beakers has shown that they held a liquid
which was rather like mead.

Beaker pottery was used in cist burials across
Britain at the beginning of the Bronze Age, but it
was not long before the Shetlanders began to
make their own versions. These were much
coarser than the 'real thing', but adopted the same
type of incised decoration. The Shetland pots,
known as 'food vessels', are found on domestic
sites, as well as in association with burials. The
pottery fragments found in cists under the
transitional Muckle Heog East cairn may be part
of a 'food vessel' rather than a true 'beaker'.
Shetlanders also made larger versions of the
beakers, which archaeologists refer to as 'urns'.
Like the food vessels, urns have been found in
houses but were also used to contain cremations.

Tongues of flame

Cremation was another entirely new practice
which took hold all over Britain during the
Bronze Age. It was not the most obvious custom
to introduce into Shetland at a time when the
woodland was so dramatically reduced.
Evidence from the hearths at the Scord of
Brouster and elsewhere demonstrates that the
population had turned to using peat as a fuel at
home, presumably because wood was becoming
too precious to burn. Recent experiments at Old
Scatness have shown that temperatures in excess
of 950°C can be generated by using bellows
when burning peat, but it would be difficult to
imagine how a pyre could be constructed which
burnt evenly using peat.

A funeral pyre is more likely to have been
constructed with more-or-less level rows of logs
with spaces between, each row set at right

angles to the one below. The spaces would then have been filled with brushwood. Once the fire was lit, it should have burnt evenly, so that the whole pyre would fall slowly downwards, keeping the body horizontal as it did so. The process would have taken at least a whole day, and if the wind changed direction, the body would have burnt unevenly, some parts possibly remaining unburnt. Where a body was left exposed for some time prior to burning the cremation would be easier, as more flesh would have decayed. The pyre may have been built using driftwood, but driftwood was often waterlogged, and so difficult to burn.

Very high temperatures were required in order to burn the stomach and chest because of the amounts of fatty tissue in these areas. The light colour of the cremated bone found in a pot at Upper Scalloway suggests that the body burnt at a temperature in excess of 800°C, similar to the temperatures achieved in a modern crematorium. The fuel ash slag found in the pot suggests that the temperatures achieved were closer to 1200°C. In some cases, bronze objects,

either worn by, or placed on, the body had melted and fused to the bones. To date, we have not found a burning site in Shetland.

The remains of a Bronze Age cremation will usually weigh considerably less than those of a modern cremation; the people who carried out the burial were apparently not too concerned about gathering up all the remains. Also, unlike a modern cremation, after which any bone is cremulated (crushed up), Bronze Age remains included recognizable chunks of bone.

Cremated remains were buried either in or under a cinerary urn (32), either a beaker-like pottery urn or an urn carved from steatite. Each urn was usually covered by a flat stone. Urns have been found both in groups and singly. A group of twenty urns was found in natural hollows around the summit of a hill in Uyea, North Mainland. Single-urn burials may be part of a larger group which did not survive.

The cremated remains found at Upper Scalloway were in a barrel-shaped pot placed

32 Cremation urn *in situ*, Upper Scalloway. (Val Turner)

upright in a shallow scoop cut into the decayed bedrock. The pot had been used for another purpose before its final function as a cremation urn, and had been broken. It was repaired by drilling three pairs of holes, one of each pair on either side of the break, and then tying them together with a strip of leather or a string of plant material. By the time of the excavation the thread had long since disappeared. The pot was found covered with a rectangular sandstone slab and seemed to contain the fairly complete remains of an adult of indeterminate sex, aged between 30 and 40 years. A similar pot to that from Scalloway was found in a short cist in Quarff, south of Lerwick. In this case, the cist itself was full of cremated bone.

There does not seem to be a clear distinction between burial and cremation traditions. A two-storey cist was found at Asta (Central Mainland). The upper level was disturbed, but it contained two steatite urns and a young adult. The contents of the lower compartment included the burnt bone of an adult and the unburnt bone of a child of 3–4 years old.

Rings of stone

One group of Shetland monuments which has never been archaeologically investigated consists of rings of stone, some of which are turf-covered, and others set into turf banks. They often have stones or a cairn in the centre. The rings may enclose cremation cemeteries and may be Bronze Age cairns. The best examples of cairns can be seen in Fetlar, at Haltadans (**33**) and nearby at the Fidlers Crus.

Haltadans has an outer ring of twenty-two low serpentine stones, inside which there is a bank formed by scooping up the earth between it and the stone ring. Two stones stand in the centre of the monument. The cairn has attracted many stories and legends, one of the most popular of which is that the stones were a group of trows

33 Haltadans, Fetlar. (RCAHMS)

(Shetland trolls). Trows come out at night, are mischievous rather than bad and, like Shetlanders, enjoy dancing and fiddle music. They must, however, stay underground during daylight hours. Unfortunately the trows at Haltadans were so busy merry-making that they did not notice the sun coming up. As a result they all turned to stone, the fiddler and his wife being the two stones in the centre. The three Fidlers Crus, close by, survive as turf-covered banks, each forming one point of an isosceles triangle.

The Rounds of Tivla in Unst are harder to find. They are three sets of circular banks, one of which consists of three concentric turf-covered rings and a central stony spread. The stone ring or enclosure at Wormadale may also be a Bronze Age cairn, and it is possible that less regular 'rings' or enclosures such as Battle Pund in Out Skerries and Housa Voe in Papa Stour may also have enclosed cremation cemeteries.

Boiled or steamed?

There are over 300 recorded mounds of fist-sized, burnt, shattered stones on the Shetland Sites and Monuments Record (34). The stones are shattered because they have been subjected to dramatic temperature changes, for instance from being heated in a fire and then being plunged into cold water. The mounds tend to be crescent-shaped, with a pit, often lined with flat stone slabs, situated between the two 'horns' of the crescent (35). The largest burnt mound in Shetland is found in Fair Isle and is 30m (99ft) long by 20m (66ft) and stands over 3m (10ft) high.

None of the burnt mounds are found in locations above 100m (330ft) and most are low-lying, situated on land which is boggy or unfavourable in a local context. By contrast, they are often adjacent to very good land. They are all close to sources of fresh water – a burn, a spring or the water table. Some burnt mounds occur in isolation; others occur in groups. A third type overlie structures which were associated with them. The burnt mound at the Ness of Sound, Lerwick, overlay a structure

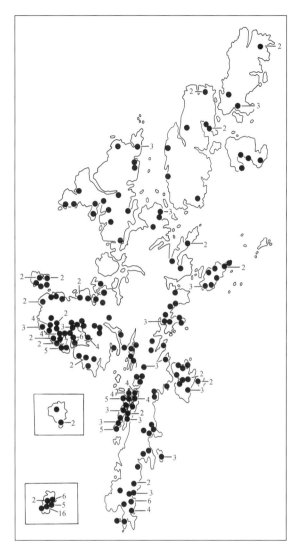

34 Burnt mounds in Shetland. (Anna Purdy)

which the excavator described as an 'oval house'. More recently, excavation revealed paving beneath the shore burnt mound at Trowie Loch, Nesting. Unfortunately, tides and the water table hampered excavation. The two mounds at Trowie Loch, another at Benston, also in Nesting, and those at Kebister were all within 300m (1000ft) of Bronze Age settlement.

Burnt mounds are usually interpreted as cooking sites although, as experiments at an excavated burnt mound at Tangwick suggest, this is not a very efficient method of cooking. The cooking theory suggests that stones were

35 The Ness of Sound burnt mound under excavation.
    The burnt stones covered an associated structure and
    a central trough of slabs on end (foreground).
    (Shetland Museum)

and 400 times. Burnt stones are also found in later domestic contexts, inside Iron Age and Norse houses. In these cases, stones were heated in fires and placed into ovens, in order to create a dry heat for cooking.

Some archaeologists suggest that isolated burnt mounds mark the kill sites of hunted animals. The flaws in this suggestion are the repeated use of the sites, the consistent choice of site (close to fresh water, just off good land), and the general lack of wild animals available for hunting in Shetland's Bronze Age. In Fair Isle, where there are twenty-eight burnt mounds, no hunter could ever be much further than 5km (3 miles) from home!

Burnt mounds may have been isolated because they were used for messy or unpleasant purposes, such as tanning or dying, which used urine and so would have been smelly. Other possible uses include fulling or felting, or alternatively sweat baths or saunas (an entirely practical method of delousing). In such a case, stones would have been heated and water from the trough sprinkled on to them in order to create steam. This would have required some form of structure, albeit a light tent of skins, to contain the steam. The group of six burnt mounds at Kebister surrounds a central area which may have contained a structure or tent.

There may be no single 'right' answer to the problem of what burnt mounds were used for; each may have had more than one purpose.

Industrial Tangwick?

The burnt mound at Tangwick, Eshaness, is situated on boggy grassland at the edge of the sea, which covers it in bad weather. It was excavated by Hazel Moore and Graeme Wilson, who discovered that originally there had been an earlier mound of burnt stone and ashy soil with no trace of an associated structure. Later, a sophisticated, purpose-built, Bronze Age industrial complex, which continued to use burnt mound technology, was built on the seaward side of the mound.

heated in a fire and placed into a trough full of water. Gradually the heat of the stones brought the water to the boil (**colour plate 5**). The disadvantage of this method of cooking was the slow, laborious process of bringing the water to the boil. The surface area of the tank was so great in comparison with its volume that a large amount of the heat generated was constantly lost. By the time the water boiled, the tank was half full of stone and very ashy. It has been calculated that each boiling used about half a cubic metre (18 cubic inches) of stone and that the average burnt mound was used between 40

The structure consisted of eight small cells arranged around a sloping paved pathway. The northern cells were built into the earlier mound. One of the northern cells was beehive-shaped and had been used as a hearth and possibly also as a kiln. The mound contained large quantities of Bronze Age pottery which may have come from the kiln. The pathway, or 'chute', sloped away from this cell to a stone-lined tank dug into the peat at the southern end. The paving stones of the chute are fire-cracked, and it seems probable that stones were heated in the fire, then rolled down the slope into the tank. The bottom of the tank lay below the water table. It was sealed with clay on three sides, but the northern edge was left unsealed, possibly to allow it to fill with water naturally, but not drain from the other end. Beside the tank was a flat stone which looks like a stone 'kneeling mat'.

The building was modified several times. Cells were blocked or altered, and a smaller box was set into the southern end of the tank. This may have served to hold pots (of food?) upright. When the burnt mound was abandoned, the tank was sealed with a slab. Later, the structure collapsed and the burnt mound material fell in from outside it.

Cellars and refrigerators

The autumn harvests had to be stored for use during the winter months. Autumn was also the best time to slaughter cattle for meat in order to avoid some of the problems of winter housing and feeding. Meat was salted (with salt obtained by boiling seawater) to help preserve it, but it then needed to be stored.

During the late Bronze Age, Shetlanders began to construct underground storage facilities known as souterrains (from the French for 'underground') or, formerly, 'earth houses' (**36**). A souterrain is a narrow underground passage ending in a slightly larger chamber, presumably the storage area. The passages were 0.6–1m (2–3ft) high, and about 0.6m (2ft) wide.

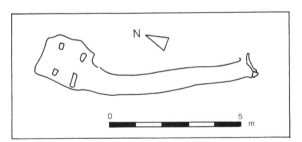

36 Inside a souterrain (plan of Jarlshof souterrain in insert from above). (Joanna Richards)

Their length varied from 2m (7ft) to 8.5m (28ft) or more, before ending in a chamber; the passages usually curved. Several souterrains have been discovered and they are often reported as 'secret tunnels', because the uncovered flagstones are above a hollow space.

The entrances to souterrains were usually inside a house, although the remains of the house may since have been destroyed. Four souterrains have been excavated in Shetland: three at Jarlshof and one at Underhoull, Unst. Visitors can still crawl into two of the souterrains at Jarlshof. The entrance at Underhoull was lintelled, and the passage went back into the hill which rose gently behind the house. The entrance area was paved with flagstones, both inside and out. At two of the Jarlshof souterrains access was via rough steps; the third was entered through a vertical shaft.

At Underhoull the passage described a semicircle; at Jarlshof one passage turned a sharp corner. The sides of the Underhoull passage were cut into rotted bedrock. Where the rock was loose or unstable, the sides were revetted with large stones or courses of flat stones, which helped to support the roof slabs. The walls of the Jarlshof souterrains comprised both upright slabs and horizontal courses. The floors of the passages were usually unpaved, sometimes sloping away from the entrance. The chambers were usually a little wider than the passage, and some had additional pillars to support the roof. The empty chamber would have been the only area wide enough for an adult to turn round comfortably.

Two of the souterrains at Jarlshof are in the bronze smith's house. One of these curved around the fire and would have been an excellent place to store grain. The fire would have kept the grain dry and prevented it from sprouting. There were few finds from the souterrain, although a rectangular plate from a bronze pendant and a fragment of a mould had been dropped inside. There were also a few animal bones.

The second souterrain was built later, and lay outside the house; this would have been better for storing meat, where cold was an advantage. The owners might even have collected ice and put it in amongst the meat to help keep it cold: one of Shetland's first refrigerators? This souterrain contained few finds other than animal bones which had been smashed in order to extract the marrow, and the hammer stones and pebbles which may have been used to smash them.

The third souterrain at Jarlshof was constructed in an Early Iron Age roundhouse, which was adapted when the souterrain was built. It was abandoned while the house was still in use, and the passage used as a refuse dump. One of the finds associated with the souterrain, when it was in use, was bone from a marine mammal which had been butchered with a sharp pointed tool. The Underhoull souterrain was also associated with an Iron Age settlement; fragments of broch pottery were found in the midden material dumped in the entrance after it was abandoned.

Bronze

By the time that bronze was found in any quantity in Shetland, dating from around 700 BC, the rest of Britain was beginning to work in iron.

Bronze is an alloy of copper and tin. There are several outcrops of copper in Shetland, although there is no evidence that any of them were worked in prehistoric times (any such evidence may, of course, have been destroyed by later working). There are certainly respectable seams of copper in Vidlin (East Mainland) and Fair Isle. Acquiring tin would have presented difficulties, as Cornwall is the only source in Britain. This may explain why there are no early styles of bronze objects known from Shetland. Alternatively, bronze may have been imported, but being too precious to discard, would have been reused. So far, however, we have not found any early bronzeworking sites where such reworking might have taken place, although a smith was reusing scrap bronze at a later date at Jarlshof (37).

As Shetland was effectively in recession, and things were probably getting steadily worse

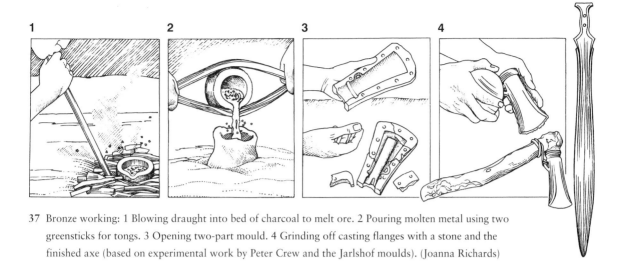

37 Bronze working: 1 Blowing draught into bed of charcoal to melt ore. 2 Pouring molten metal using two greensticks for tongs. 3 Opening two-part mould. 4 Grinding off casting flanges with a stone and the finished axe (based on experimental work by Peter Crew and the Jarlshof moulds). (Joanna Richards)

throughout the Bronze Age, the opportunities for trade or long-distance import were doubtless limited. The amount of bronze found from sites in Shetland increases around 700 BC, the end of the Bronze Age. As iron was becoming increasingly common in the rest of Britain, so bronze was becoming less valuable, which might explain why it was found more readily. Iron replaced some of the previous uses of bronze, although bronze continued to be used for objects such as swords and jewellery.

Around 700 BC a bronze smith, trained in the Irish tradition of bronzeworking, arrived at Jarlshof and set up a workshop in a recently abandoned house. He or she built a large hearth in the centre of the house, using an upright slab for a fire back. The fire was sheltered from the wind with a screen of hides. The finds from the workshop included bone awls, chisels and clay moulds; one mould for casting a V-type bronze sword was complete. There was also a store of carbonized wood, including oak, pine, willow, hazel and birch, some of which was certainly driftwood. The cache was probably charcoal, prepared for smelting.

After a hiatus during which parts of the building were remodelled, the smith continued work at a large circular hearth which was constructed on a bed of gravel covered in clay. This hearth was also backed with a large upright stone and was covered in peat ash to a depth of 0.5m (20in). Behind the fire back, a triangular structure of flagstones, surrounded by soil burnt brick red, was probably the site of a furnace or kiln. An air duct or flue extended for 2m (6ft) south from the area.

The adjacent house may also have been used as a smithy after it had been abandoned as a dwelling. It had a central fireplace, and there was a hollow filled with sand which probably held the moulds upright during the casting process. Large numbers of clay mould fragments were discovered in the house, including moulds for at least eight socketed axes, seven swords and a sunflower pin.

Fragments of two types of moulds were found at Jarlshof: two-part moulds and moulds for *cire-perdue*. Two-part moulds comprised two halves which could be taken apart. These moulds were usually only used once (38). Stone moulds were more durable and could have been reused. If the object was to be hollow, such as a socketed axe, a central core would have to be suspended in position when the mould was standing upright in sand during casting. When two-part moulds were removed, the bronze object would have had a rim of surplus metal around the line of the join. This had to be chipped or filed away before the finished object was polished.

38 Fragments of clay moulds used to make a bronze axe, found at Jarlshof. (National Museums of Scotland)

Cire-perdue (lost wax) moulds were used to make casting rods. First of all, a wax model was made of the object. The model was then covered in clay. When the clay was fired, the wax melted and trickled out, allowing space for the molten metal to be poured in. These moulds had to be smashed in order to get the object out. The broken fragments found at Jarlshof had been thrown into a small disused chamber and passage, both of which were already covered in sand, blown in after they were abandoned.

Fragments of crucibles, the clay containers used to hold the metal as it melted, were also found on the site together with slag, the waste product of smithing.

A new dawn

Wiltrow lies a little to the north-west of Jarlshof. While Alexander Curle was digging at Jarlshof in the 1930s, he took time off to excavate an oval house at Wiltrow (**39**). The house itself was a typical oval house with an inner chamber. About 3m (10ft) from the house, Curle discovered three furnaces which had been used to smelt bog iron. The stone tools which were found associated with the iron smelting were similar to the tools found at Jarlshof, but

39 Excavation at Wiltrow, 1935. (RCAHMS)

some were encrusted with iron, which proves that they were contemporary with the smithing. Although the two sites were closely related in time, Wiltrow dates to the onset of a new set of customs and practices, which archaeologists call the 'Iron Age'.

Each furnace at Wiltrow was formed by directing a draught along a flue to a 'throttle', which was formed by converging stones and covered by a slab. Each flue ended in a peat fire, or furnace, and each faced a different direction (north, east and west), presumably to take advantage of the wind direction. The northern flue was best preserved: a narrow channel

1.25m (4ft) long and 15cm (6in) wide, lined with stones on either side. At 0.53m (21in) from the outer end of the flue, a flat triangular stone could be slotted into either side, to act as a shutter closing the flue. Beyond each flue was a chamber, the floor of which was covered in peat ash. An opening in the south wall led into another chamber which contained a quantity of bog ore and was probably a store-room. The finds from the site included a sandstone 'tuyere', the spout of a bellows for increasing the draught into the furnace (40).

40 Ironworking: 1 Goatskin bellows blowing draught into bloomery. 2 Bloom smithing with wooden mallet and anvil. 3 Iron being consolidated on a stone anvil with an iron hammer. 4 Smithing of doubled bar (based on experimental work by Peter Crew and site at Wiltrow). (Joanna Richards)

The introduction of iron coincided with a period of change in Shetland. For the first time people needed to protect themselves with fortifications, but the ability to do this indicates a degree of affluence, an impression supported by the fact that metal was becoming more abundant. During the early centuries AD the weather became milder, and the economy appears to have begun to stabilize. Later in the Iron Age, precious metals began to appear in Shetland.

6
Gateways to the sea?

The beginning of the Iron Age (around 500 BC) was a turning point in Shetland's history: people began to build fortifications. Perhaps access to iron weapons made life more dangerous; perhaps there were more people living in Shetland than the land could comfortably support, with the result that those who had assets needed to defend them. The majority of excavated sites from this period are either forts or broch sites (**41**). Undefended sites remain more elusive, although one has recently been excavated at Bayanne, in Yell.

Forts or brochs: chickens or eggs?

We have very little evidence about the relationship between forts and brochs: whether they were contemporary and, if not, which came first. At Clickhimin there is clear evidence that a fort was built before a broch. This is the only site from which archaeologists have clear dating evidence for a building sequence. There is slim evidence for suggesting that forts and brochs were occupied at the same time, based on the type of pottery found at the Ness of Burgi, excavated in the 1930s. The evidence from Clickhimin, and also other sites where brochs have been built inside what may once have been fort ramparts (for example, Burland and Aithsetter), is perhaps more compelling.

Clickhimin blockhouse fort

Clickhimin is situated on a peninsula which today protrudes into the Loch of Clickhimin, on the south side of Lerwick (**42**). Initially it was

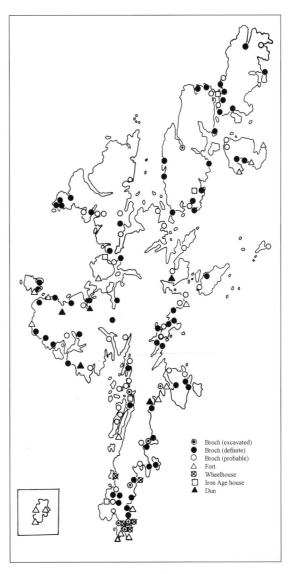

41 Iron Age Shetland. (Anna Purdy)

42 The Clickhimin peninsula, showing the remains of the Bronze Age farmstead (back, right), the blockhouse fort (left) and the later broch (centre), all surrounded by an early Iron Age wall. (RCAHMS)

the site of a Bronze Age farmstead. The farmstead was occupied for a long period, and continued in use as life on the peninsula began to change.

The first major alteration arose when people dug a ditch across the neck of the peninsula and erected a wall around the site. Wooden lean-to buildings were constructed around the inside of the wall. Around 100 BC a large stone 'gatehouse' or 'blockhouse' was erected. The blockhouse formed the entrance through the wall which encircled an area at the end of the peninsula. The massive stone front concealed a two-storey wooden building attached to the rear. The upper floor seems to have been residential, whilst animals were stalled on the ground floor beneath. The blockhouse wall was not bonded into the encircling peninsular wall and so the two structures, although contemporary, must have been built independently. A similar fort on an island in the Loch of Huxter, in Whalsay, has a blockhouse still attached to the ring wall. The joints between these are not bonded either. Later, the wall of the ring fort at Clickhimin was enlarged, and as a result the blockhouse was left free-standing and an outer staircase was

1 Protecting the ard marks at Old Scatness, formed where the ard plough cut into the subsoil. (Shetland Amenity Trust)

2 Heel-shaped chambered cairn, Vementry. (Shetland Museum)

3 Cup-marked stone, Belmont. (Shetland Amenity Trust)

4 Shetland Knives. (Shetland Museum)

5 Burnt-mound cooking experiment in fully excavated tank at Tangwick. (Deborah Lamb)

6 Clickhimin blockhouse (foreground) and broch (behind). (Historic Scotland)

7 Culswick Broch, constructed of sandstone with a triangular door lintel. (Shetland Museum)

8 Wheelhouses within the broch courtyard at Jarlshof, with the aisled house in the foreground. (Historic Scotland)

9 'Chessmen' from Mail, Cunningsburgh (left) and Upper Scalloway. (Niall Sharples)

10 St Ninian's Isle chapel.
    (Val Turner, Shetland
    Amenity Trust)

11 Part of the St Ninian's Isle
    Treasure (two bowls, three cones,
    one brooch, two sword chapes,
    three brooches.
    (National Museums of Scotland)

12 A monastic site at the Birrier of West
 Sandwick. (Val Turner/Eddie Watt,
 Shetland Amenity Trust)

13 The earliest Viking or Norse house site
 at Jarlshof, with later Norse structures
 to the east (right). (Historic Scotland)

14 (a) and (b) Reroofing a horizontal mill using techniques which have probably been used in Shetland for 5000 years. A lattice of ropes is strung across a wooden framework, and turves are laid, grass side down, on top. Straw thatching is laid over the top and secured with further ropes, weighted by stones. (Shetland Amenity Trust)

15 The Iron Age village which surrounds the broch site at Old Scatness
at the end of the 1997 excavation season. (Steve Dockrill)

added. Kinks visible in the wall show where it was extended.

The Clickhimin blockhouse wall curves along its 13m (43ft) length and stood at least two storeys high (**colour plate 6**). It is 4.1m (13.5ft) thick with an entrance passage a little over 1m (4ft) wide passing through the centre at ground level. The passageway is low; anyone entering would have to stoop in order to reach the door which, in common with broch entrances, is halfway along the passage. The door would have opened inwards and could have been locked against intruders from the inside by a bar inserted into holes on either side of the doorway. There was a cell, possibly for storage, or possibly structural, on each side of the passage. The cells had no ground-level access and could only have been entered from the floor above.

Today the Clickhimin blockhouse wall stands over 3m (10ft) high (**43**). On its inside face there is a 'scarcement', a ledge of projecting slabs. This would have supported the upper floor of the wooden building which also had a cobbled ground floor. The ring wall

around the peninsula supported lean-to buildings; these probably housed more people as well as serving as byres.

J. R. C. Hamilton, who excavated Clickhimin in the 1950s, thought that the blockhouse was the house of a chieftain, as similar strongholds were described in the Irish epics. In these epics the chieftain lived beside the gate, the showpiece of the settlement. Some of today's scholars agree that the Irish epics included genuine folk memories of prehistoric times. There were clearly contacts between people from Jarlshof and Ireland by Bronze Age times, and it is perhaps not too far-fetched to suggest that Shetlandic and Irish societies may have been organized in similar ways. In the nineteenth century a 'footprint stone' was discovered at Clickhimin. It had a pair of life-size feet cut into it, and was built into the later causeway. Hamilton related this to clan coronation practices in Ireland which used similar stones, and thought that this might be further evidence of contact between Shetlandic and Irish nobility.

43 The blockhouse, Clickhimin. (Historic Scotland)

If the blockhouse was the house of a Shetlandic chieftain, this would certainly explain why it continued to be used even after the wall-line was changed.

During the first or second centuries BC, environmental 'disaster' struck Clickhimin when the peninsula flooded. Almost overnight the promontory became an islet and the area of usable land was reduced. The ring wall had to be buttressed in places and many of the buildings around it had to be demolished, but the blockhouse survived intact.

What happened next is unclear. Hamilton thought that the inhabitants began to build a smaller ring wall around the island, but before they got very far with the building the community had a change of heart. More recently it has been suggested that what Hamilton interpreted as rebuilding was, in fact, the remains of the buttress of a first attempt at broch building which collapsed. Archaeologists would need to be able to dig underneath the existing broch in order to resolve this question, but the fact remains that the blockhouse became replaced by a broch. The number of similarities between broch and fort construction indicates both that there was a fairly short period of time between the construction of the two and that the fort and broch builders were closely related groups, if not one and the same people.

Other blockhouses

The fort standing on an island in the Loch of Huxter, Whalsay, seems to have been very similar to the original fort at Clickhimin. The Huxter fort was reached by a causeway which is still the only means of approach on foot. In 1879 the Huxter fort stood to much the same height as Clickhimin does now and had the characteristic passageway with a doorway in the centre and chambers on either side. Unfortunately, at the same time that Huxter was recorded it was in the process of being 'cleared of loose stone' (dismantled!) in order to build a school (A. Mitchell writing in the *Proceedings of the Society of Antiquaries of Scotland*, 1880–1).

44 Ness of Burgi blockhouse fort as it may have looked 2000 years ago. (Joanna Richards)

The blockhouses at Scatness and the Ness of Burgi lie close together on the Scat Ness peninsula at the southern extremity of Shetland Mainland (**44**). Each blockhouse stands behind the bank cutting off the neck of the peninsula on which it is situated, rather like the later phase at Clickhimin. In the banks at Scatness there is a gap, probably the entrance, which was at least 9.5m (31ft) wide – extraordinarily wide if the entrance was intended to be defensive.

One side of the Scatness blockhouse had eroded into the sea before it was excavated in 1983. What remains stands only 1.6m (5ft) high. In the remaining side there appears to have been an external staircase and two internal cells, one cell opening from the other and entered through a passage from the seaward face of the blockhouse. The blockhouse was later buttressed within the cells, so blocking the access between them. After this the western cell could only be entered from above. The buttressing and rebuilding indicate the presence of an upper level which was of more significance than the lower level, which does not seem to have been heavily used.

Burgi Geos is situated on a remote, precipitous peninsula in Yell and resembles one side of the other blockhouses, the entranceway and second side apparently never having been built (**45**). The approach path passes beside the structure, not through it, and appears to continue on to another structure, only visible as an area of darker vegetation, further along the peninsula. There never seems to have been any more to the structure, although it is situated very close to the eroding cliff top. A ring wall projects from the blockhouse, enclosing a tiny area, extending only 4m (13ft) back from the rear of the building. An area of vegetation change within the enclosure suggests that there are building foundations below the surface.

The approach to Burgi Geos is extremely unusual. The path descends into a narrow dip, then climbs the peninsula on the other side. On

Sketched Aug 18 1853. Ancient Brough (fortification) on the Burgie Goes West Neips North Yell

45 Burgi Geos (sketch 1853). (RCAHMS)

the north side the descent is lined by boulders on end; on the south side it is bounded by a mound and bank which follows the edge of the path and is set with jagged stones on end. These stones resemble *chevaux de frise*, a defensive structure which would normally be aligned *across* an approach, in order to hinder access, rather than being aligned beside the path. The nearest examples of real *chevaux de frise* are in south-east Scotland and around the Irish Sea, and are merely stone copies of a structure which is more usually constructed using wooden stakes. Lamb thinks that the builders of Burgi Geos had seen *chevaux de frise* elsewhere, known that they were defensive and that they went outside the fort, but got them the wrong way round!

Blockhouses or gateways?

It is impossible to get inside the minds of previous generations and to decide what prompted them to do what they did. The excavations at Scatness and the Ness of Burgi revealed no evidence of timber buildings attached to the back of the blockhouses; however, this may be a result of marine erosion. Some archaeologists have suggested that the blockhouse sites were symbolic representations either of defences or of power, allowing a group to *look* fierce, and that actual warfare was restricted to challenges between the champions of each community. The archaeological evidence for what the blockhouses *were* used for is, however, scanty. Stephen Carter (1995) suggested that the blockhouses might have been ceremonial gateways used perhaps in rites of passage. There is certainly no archaeological evidence of warfare having been launched against the blockhouses; if they were intended to frighten off adversaries, they appear to have succeeded.

If the Burgi Geos *chevaux de frise* were intended to be prestigious then it would not matter if the builders got them the wrong way round. It seems strange, however, that Burgi Geos was built a kilometre (three-quarters of a mile) from what must have been the nearest usable land and in such a potentially dangerous location. Perhaps the intention never was to create *chevaux de frise*; indeed, the position of the stones actually assists the visitor to approach the blockhouse safely.

The location of Burgi Geos is so remote, and so potentially treacherous, that the chances of its ever being excavated and revealing its secrets are, regrettably, equally remote. By contrast, the Ness of Burgi and Scatness blockhouses were situated at the heart of Iron Age activity in the fertile South Mainland.

The Norse word 'borg' meant 'strong place' or 'fortification', and it is from this that the word 'broch' is derived. The names Ness of Burgi and Burgi Geos indicate that the Norse settlers to Shetland understood the blockhouses to be fortifications. The pottery evidence from the Ness of Burgi, and also from Scatness, suggests that the abandonment and collapse, or stone robbing, happened late in the Iron Age. The Norse perceptions of the blockhouses, however, are still likely to be more accurate than our own, as they were far closer in time.

The theories of blockhouses as places of show and display may well contain some truth, but the effects of coastal erosion, the similarities between forts and brochs, the place-name evidence and the sheer effort that went into building the forts, together with evidence from Clickhimin, not to mention other promontory forts, all indicate that the truth is somewhat more complicated. To abandon all consideration of association between the blockhouses and defence would be to overstate the case somewhat.

Promontory forts

Every blockhouse site was associated either with walls or with a series of banks which cut off the promontory. There are at least twenty other sites which have banks across the landward ends of promontories; eight of these also contain brochs.

The promontories at Landberg, Fair Isle, and at Hog Island, Nesting, each have a series of three low banks and an inner, stone-revetted

rampart. The ramparts at Landberg have an entrance passing through all three banks, beyond which there is a steep climb up on to the main rampart and the promontory. John Hunter's recent excavation suggests that the ramparts originally stood 2m (6ft) high. The ramparts were created by digging ditches into the rock and building with the excavated material. They were finished off with huge boulders which were placed on top.

Behind the inner rampart is a later structure which John Hunter believes to be a chapel site. Geophysical survey on the promontory showed a ditch which appears to follow the northern edge of the promontory. Excavation revealed a vertical-sided rock-cut gallery over 1m (3ft) deep. Further excavation will demonstrate whether the gallery does run along the length of the peninsula, or whether it curves, possibly being part of a rock-cut souterrain.

The Hog Island fort (46) was cut in two by the sea, the main stone-revetted rampart being on the far side of the eroded drop. As at Landberg, the main rampart overlooks the lower dump banks, which might have done little more than slow down any attackers. Elsewhere, promontories are cut off not by banks but by stone walls, usually only identifiable in cliff edge sections.

Some promontory forts appeared to have contained the remains of buildings. In 1774, George Low described a fort at Sumburgh Head: 'at the entrance, still observable the foundation of a large house, which probably served as a guardroom, along the wall, and at some distance, the marks of numerous small buildings'.

At the broch of Burland there are three lines of defensive bank with a central entrance through them all. The inner bank has a wall at the west side with a well-finished end face. If the broch was not apparent, the site could easily be classified as a 'probable blockhouse', together with similar sites at the Holm of Copister in Yell and Fugla Ness in the North Mainland. The defensive banks, however, may have been integral to the broch structure. The foundations

46 Hog Island, promontory fort. (Historic Scotland)

on the promontory at the Ness of Garth, Sandness, resemble those found on later monastic sites, for example, Strandibrough, Fetlar, and the later structure at Landberg which may also have been a chapel site, indicating the reuse of defended promontories.

Raymond Lamb has suggested that the concept of promontory forts was not indigenous to Shetland because dump ramparts are not the obvious method of construction when the bedrock is so close to the surface, but this would beg the question of where they did originate. Certainly, building in turf or stone would have been far easier.

7
Towers of strength

The most visible sites in the Shetland landscape are the brochs. In 1855, Sir Henry Dryden listed seventy-five broch sites in Shetland, and this was before the discovery of the brochs at Jarlshof, Upper Scalloway and Old Scatness, to name but a few. If place-name evidence is taken into account, the number of probable broch sites now stands at over 120. Brochs are found only in Scotland. There are about 500 in all, most of which occur in the Northern and Western Isles; Shetland has the highest density.

The term 'broch' refers to a round tower with massive inner and outer stone walls which are hollow above the first floor. The gap between the walls narrows as they become higher, and the two are 'tied' together with stones which pass from one wall to the other. This strengthened the structure and allowed the broch builders to employ less stone than if it were solid, as well as creating galleries which could be used for storage. Brochs have only one small entrance, no windows, stairs within the walls, scarcements which probably helped to support timber floors, and cells within the ground-level walls (other than in rare, non-Shetland, cases where these are also hollow).

The broch at Mousa was reused as a defensive refuge during Viking times. The *Orkneyinga Saga* describes the elopement of Margaret, mother of Earl Harald, with Erlend from Orkney to Shetland in AD 1153. The couple took refuge in the broch at

'Moseyjarborg'. They were pursued by Harald and his men, who laid siege to the broch, but the saga records that they found it 'an unhandy place to attack'. As a result the two sides came to an agreement and Earl Harald gave his consent to the marriage!

Leading dry-stone expert Richard Tufnell studied the way in which the brochs were constructed. Most were built either on to bedrock or on a platform of boulder clay which was resistant to settling. The foundation course was wider than the wall of the broch above ground. The faces of brochs were usually well finished, and where the walls of a broch still stand today, the faces are largely intact. The core behind the face was well packed; the better packed it was, the better the broch stands today. Brochs could have been constructed as vertical towers, but the inward-sloping, outer face of the lower levels (the batter) meant that the broch could be built higher in comparison with the base area. This characteristic batter is very clear in the broch at Mousa.

In contrast to many of the other brochs, that at Culswick on the West Side was built of large irregular blocks of red and white granite with a spectacular triangular lintel over the door (**colour plate 7**). In 1774 it stood 7m (23ft) high, and even then George Low wrote that 'many of the stones have been removed for house-building'. Today Culswick is far lower, but its dramatic impact is still obvious from the sea.

Mousa

Of all the brochs, Mousa (47) is the most impressive which survives today, still standing 13m (43ft) high (see **cover photo**). In 1859 Sir Henry Dryden became concerned about the state of the fabric of the broch, which 'according to the recent Report of a practical Architect, is likely to go rapidly into ruin unless its decay is arrested by timely and judicious repairs'. He launched an appeal for subscriptions from Fellows of the Society of Antiquaries of Scotland. Sir Henry and Mr Bruce, who owned Mousa, made up the deficit, and the top of the wall was levelled, 'two parts of it having fallen down,

measuring about nine feet in length by five feet in height'. An etching of the broch in its 'dilapidated' state, reproduced in the *Proceedings of the Society of Antiquaries*, shows that the bulk of the broch stood then to the same height as it does today. The work was presumably carried out, although no report seems to have been made to the Society. In 1921, when the broch was taken into the care of the Ministry of Works, further clearance and repairs were undertaken. Neither of these episodes added to the overall height of the broch, and local tales of the broch being built up considerably in, or since, Victorian times have no substance.

The wall thickness of Mousa is similar to that of the other brochs in Shetland; the difference lies

47 Mousa Broch (RCAHMS)

in the smaller overall diameter: 15m (49ft) rather than 20m (66ft), with an inner court only 6m (20ft) wide. This meant that the foundations were extremely solid, and could carry a tower which was taller than average. We do not know whether Mousa's height really was exceptional; equally tall towers may have been constructed on wider bases, but have subsequently collapsed or been lowered deliberately. The dimensions of Mousa, however, together with the fact that the island is blessed with Old Red Sandstone flags, some of the best building material available in Shetland, have kept the tower standing for 2000 years.

When nineteenth-century antiquarians entered Mousa, the real entrance lay at ground level but was covered by external debris. As a result, they broke in through a cell above the entrance passage which today seems unusually high as the original roofing slabs have been removed. In typical fashion, as with the blockhouse forts, the door was halfway along the entrance passage; one of the door jambs and the slot behind it for securing the bar across the inside of the door can still be seen. This meant that originally people would have reached the door in a stooped position; hardly an ideal position for anyone mounting an attack to be in, although good for reducing the amount of draught.

In the middle of the floor at Mousa is a water tank which is cut through to bedrock. This was presumably kept topped up with water either from springs or from the loch nearby. The other stone features of the broch floor were secondary, inserted by later Iron Age inhabitants who adapted the structure. Two stone scarcements, which encircle the tower at about head height, supported wooden floors. The fronts of the floors rested on wooden posts, and people would have climbed up to them using wooden ladders. These floors may well have formed the main living areas.

The ground floor has three cells built into the otherwise solid walls. These may have been cosy places in which to sleep, or they may have been storage areas. Small fires may have been built on the raised floors rather than at ground level. If

48 The staircase within the double walls of Mousa Broch which runs up to the wall-head. (Historic Scotland)

there had been a large central fire at ground level, the broch would have been in constant danger of going up in flames. Whenever anyone opened the door, the broch could potentially have become a perfect furnace! The builders at Mousa were not sufficiently concerned about this possibility to take evasive action; the entrance to Mousa faces slightly south of west, the direction of the prevailing wind.

Opposite the entrance there is a series of weight-relieving apertures within the inner broch wall. The lowest of these allows access to the staircase which winds continuously between the inner and outer walls from 3m (10ft) above ground level to the wall-head. The apertures in the wall may have helped to light the staircase (48), which would otherwise be pitch dark. The staircase passes through some of the six galleries formed where the inner and outer walls are tied together by large slabs. Part of the original wall-head survives, allowing us to be sure of the full height of the broch, and some of the original capping, a slanting slabbed roof, is still in place. From the top of the broch there is a good view of the Sound (the stretch of water between Mousa and the Mainland). The broch is also just high enough to afford a view across the island to the sea on the other side.

There are traces of an external wall and platform around the broch, but they do not appear to have been very substantial. They have been interpreted as a stock enclosure rather than a serious attempt at defence. There were once traces of small houses close to the broch entrance, but these have since disappeared into the sea. The lack of a serious defensive wall, the lack of guard cells beside the entrance, and the height of the broch may be reasons to place Mousa late in the sequence of broch building, built for display rather than for defence. This, however, does not accord with the theory of a chain of brochs working in co-operation (see page 79). Perhaps the situation on Mousa was sufficiently protected in itself to allow its inhabitants to be less concerned with defensive banks. While this may seem improbable on a calm summer day, it should be remembered that a number of ships have foundered in the waters around the island in this century alone.

Associated buildings

Only Clickhimin has produced any buildings apparently directly contemporary with the life of the broch, and there they already existed as part of the blockhouse complex. Approximately 50 per cent of brochs had either a wall or banks and ditches on at least one side, some of which enclose the remains of buildings other than the broch. At Jarlshof the broch dwellers built a substantial house and byre within the broch courtyard. J. R. C. Hamilton thought that the builders lowered the wall at this time in order to

reuse some of the stone in the new 'aisled' house. This house was not as well built as the broch, and the builders used beach stones mixed with the faced sandstone. The byre had a roughly cobbled floor with a large drain running through it and may have housed cattle. The Jarlshof aisled house and byre were later replaced by a complex of wheelhouses, two of them built within the courtyard wall.

Upper Scalloway Broch

In 1989, house building at Upper Scalloway uncovered a medieval cemetery and sliced through a structure full of Iron Age pottery. This discovery led to what became the first modern excavation of a broch site in Shetland. Although the broch stood only two courses of stone high (49), and the north-east corner had already been destroyed by the developers, the excavation carried out by Rod McCullough in the winter of 1989 and Niall Sharples in the spring of 1990 gave us a new insight into what brochs may have been like inside. Today, although there is nothing of the site to be seen, we can tell from its prominent position on a knoll at the southern end of a ridge that the broch dwellers would have had an excellent view of any vessels entering East Voe.

All that was excavated of the broch defences was a bank and ditch to the south. The bank contained a structure which may have been a guard chamber within the rampart. The ground drops away sharply from the foot of the broch on three sides, so major defences were probably only important along the ridge to the north. Unfortunately, that area could not be excavated.

The excavators think that like Clickhimin Broch, Scalloway may not have been a perfect circle in ground plan; instead it may have been slightly oval-shaped, being rather more elongated to the east. The outer diameter of Upper Scalloway was slightly bigger than average and the inside was slightly smaller, and so the broch may have been tall and strong. Its foundations were on bedrock, which had been dug out in places.

49 Although very little remained of the Upper Scalloway
Broch, it had been built with great attention to keeping
the courses even. (Rod McCullough)

An arc of flimsy post-holes was situated
about 1.4m (4ft 6in) inside the inner wall of the
broch, leading Niall Sharples to suggest that the
broch floor area was divided by radial partitions
(50). He did not find more substantial post-
holes relating to a timber interior, probably
because the centre of the broch was removed by
later Iron Age inhabitants. There were several
pits, lined with green clay, set into the floor.
These may have been cooking pits (if there had
been a central fire), or they may have been
containers for storing water for a variety of
purposes. One of the pits contained a large
single stone which had been shaped to fit it; the
pit may have contained a dedicatory burial,
made when the broch was constructed (common
practice in Iron Age houses in the Western Isles).

The floor was covered by an organic layer,
possibly a mixture of animal fodder and straw;
this may have been due to over-wintering
animals in the broch. It is hard to imagine cattle
being brought in through the long, low, narrow
entrance of a broch, but sheep might have been
brought inside for lambing. The organic
material might, however, have been winter

50 Alan Sorrell's reconstruction of the interior of
Clickhimin broch. Ideas about the interior are gradually
changing, but the essential idea, with the wooden
platforms, still holds good. (Historic Scotland)

fodder, stored in the broch. Stephen Carter proved that the organic material on the floor had not come from the roof; he discovered that a type of worm, which lives deep in the soil, had been living in it, depositing its casts, which were burnt together with the surrounding deposits. The floor must have been damp for these particular worms to have thrived. A large quantity of barley was also found on the floor.

Fire!

Life in Upper Scalloway Broch seems to have come to an abrupt end at some time between AD 415 and 525, when, whether by accident or design, the broch caught fire. The date for the end of the broch is later than has been conventionally suggested for brochs, and by this time, Upper Scalloway may have been in use for several centuries. Once the door had burnt through, the broch may have fallen victim to the furnace effect. The wooden superstructure and the consequent collapse of the roof would have fuelled the fire. The temperatures in the burning broch exceeded 650°C, causing ash to melt and recrystallize well below the ground surface.

Where did the brochs come from?

The origin of the brochs is hotly debated in archaeological circles. Cases have been advanced for both the Western Isles and Orkney as the place where brochs developed first. In the Western Isles there are a number of structures which are not completely circular, but which resemble brochs in other respects, and which may be their precursors. In Orkney, three early Iron Age houses have been excavated (Quanterness, Bu and Howe); the walls of each had been widened after they were first built, with inner and outer faces added. This may, however, be no more than the type of modification to house shapes which was already taking place in Bronze Age Shetland. More compelling, perhaps, is the fact that the house at Howe was two storeys high, with two staircases built into the wall and guard cells at the entrance. The Howe house might have been built by someone who was

already familiar with broch building, but was unable to build one at that time, whether through lack of wealth, status, or lack of a builder, we can only speculate: in time it was replaced by a broch. The Howe house does not prove the 'Atlantic Roundhouse' theory, which suggests that a broch is merely a large house.

Nor can Shetland be entirely ruled out as a contender. The blockhouse forts found in Shetland (see chapter 6) share several characteristics with the brochs, including cells, intramural staircases, a doorway within a low stone passage, and scarcements supporting floors. At Clickhimin, the blockhouse fort was partially replaced by a broch, and although the first attempt was apparently unsuccessful, it suggests that the broch builders drew heavily on their knowledge of Shetland fort-building techniques. There was a certain logic in progressing from an arc-shaped fort to a circular broch; the rear of a timber fort would have been very vulnerable if an attacker managed to get behind it. A circular broch provided a stone shell which encased and protected the timber structures within it. The fact that the majority of Shetland brochs show a large degree of uniformity suggests that the concept of broch building was fairly well established by the time they were built; however, the broch builders must have been aware of the way the forts were built.

Duns

In addition to the brochs there are five sites known as duns. These are single-skinned towers, all smaller in diameter than the brochs, and in the main situated inland. Four of the five are on islets within lochs (for example, Brindister, near Lerwick). There have been no modern studies of any of the sites, and at present we have little idea of how they relate to the brochs or to broch development.

Why build a broch?

The building of the forts and brochs suggests that life in the Iron Age was becoming more unsettled. Both forts and brochs were often situated close to cliffs, which provided natural defences; if built to a sufficient height, they would always have commanded good sea views. Earthen ramparts and ditches, which were sometimes stone-faced, stood up to 3m (10ft) high.

As with forts, archaeologists debate to what extent brochs were primarily defensive and to what extent they were built for prestige. It would be fairly easy for attackers to lay siege to a broch, providing that they had the provisions and patience to sit it out. Brochs rarely contained wells, and stored water could not last indefinitely; neither could brochs accommodate many livestock, or serve to protect large quantities of crops, however extreme the circumstances. The attackers could hasten the capitulation of the broch inhabitants by setting the entrance alight and smoking them out. Indeed, under such conditions the low approach to the broch door could become an advantage to the attackers, who could throw brushwood and lighted fire brands into the passage without crawling in themselves.

Brochs did, however, represent a secure place of retreat if the threat was limited to that of local skirmishes, and may have acted as a deterrent to attackers. Earl Harald's men had access to better weaponry and technology than the original Iron Age residents, when they unsuccessfully attacked Mousa centuries later.

The deterioration of the climate at the end of the Bronze Age, accompanied by the spread of blanket peat, placed the cultivable land under far more pressure, which may have led to local tensions. People had to live more closely, and local hierarchies may have developed. Like the blockhouses, brochs may have been intended to demonstrate the wealth and power of the leaders, as well as providing a place of retreat in times of trouble (**51**).

51 The unexcavated broch mound at Dalsetter, South Mainland, overlain by later structures of several periods including a possible Pictish building on the broch mound itself (right of centre). (Historic Scotland)

One of the problems in attempting to establish the role of the brochs is that we do not yet know enough about their economy or about the Iron Age landscape which surrounded them. Early excavations concentrated on the towers themselves, and took place before the development of techniques which allow the examination of environmental factors. Recent work at Upper Scalloway provides a first glimpse into broch-period economics. Cattle and sheep were equally important as food, and pork was also a regular part of the diet. Barley was grown in some quantity, but fish were immature and small, being caught close to the shore. The Old Scatness Broch and Jarlshof Environs Project, currently in progress, is addressing the question of how brochs related to the surrounding environment. This is being done by using soil science, by comparing the environmental evidence from the crofting period of the excavation with what is documented from that period and then relating this backwards to the environmental evidence found from the Iron Age, and by detailed mapping of the landscape in order to discover as much as possible about the broch hinterland, what it once was and how it has developed. Noel Fojut divided the South Mainland into areas of land each surrounding a broch. He assumed that each broch would control its own parcel of land and that the brochs were the local focus of settlement. He calculated that each of these areas could grow enough grain to support at least 100 people, and perhaps as many as 483, even allowing for the fact that there may be broch sites yet to be found. Within this scenario, brochs would be the centre of small farming communities, whose houses have yet to be found.

To have a broch built would have required a degree of affluence, as both the skilled builders and the labourers, and perhaps their dependants too, would have had to have been fed and supported by the community while building was in progress. Richard Tufnell concluded that it would take an apprenticeship of several years of full-time dry-stone building in order to achieve the level of skill required to become a competent broch master craftsman. It is unlikely that each local community could have had sufficient experience within it to build a broch. The community would almost certainly have had to 'buy in' skills from an itinerant team. This suggests that despite the deteriorating climate, people were not reduced to a subsistence economy but still produced a surplus of food.

Possessions

The objects found in brochs do not indicate a particularly high-status group of people. The majority of tools were still made from stone, although some bronze was used. The pottery styles were a little more elaborate than they had previously been; basic bucket-shaped pots gave way to pots which were more vase-shaped and had out-turned rims. At the height of the broch period, some of the pots had decorative bands of twisted or finger-pinched clay added to them. A new type of red-brown fabric was introduced, together with a fine black fabric which was burnished to give a glossy shine to the outside. It may be that different fabrics were put to different uses. The heavier pots, tempered with steatite, were probably cooking pots, while the black burnished pottery may have been the dinner service! At Scalloway fragments of two steatite pots of a type normally thought to be Norse were clearly broch period.

There has been little jewellery found, other than a bone and stone bead necklace and a ring-headed pin from Upper Scalloway. Two of the more unusual objects from Scalloway indicate contact with what was happening on the British mainland. A copper alloy bowl and a group of miniature tools are both Roman in origin, although it seems that they were lost at Scalloway two to three centuries after they were manufactured. A sword pommel of Roman origin was lost outside the broch in the first or second centuries AD. It is also possible that the black burnished broch pottery may have been a deliberate attempt to copy the extremely fine black burnished ware made by the Romans. It

52 Dice, one of which is loaded, from Upper Scalloway. (Niall Sharples)

was not until the Scalloway Broch was going out of use that the surviving objects become more elaborate and jewellery becomes more evident.

Broch life was not all work and no play. Four bone dice were found in Upper Scalloway Broch; one of them was loaded with a small pin! This dice was rolled fifty times in an experiment; it came to rest at '5' thirty-two times, and at '6' only once (52)!

Situation

Since the brochs were in prominent positions they were more vulnerable to the elements than earlier structures, which tended to hug the ground and used earth, turf and midden material as insulation. Brochs also required a large amount of timber in a landscape where wood was scarce.

The Shetland brochs are all built along the coast and clearly have an important relationship both with it and with each other. They are situated in positions which command good views along the coasts and voes. At 7–13m high (23–43ft), even the brochs which are slightly inland, such as Houlland in Eshaness, would

afford a good coastal view from the top. The defensive advantage of being situated in the loch must have outweighed the need to build it on the cliff top, where it could afford a much better view at a lower height. There is good access to the wall-head at Mousa, and there is no case for saying that this was unusual as there are no other complete brochs. It may have been achieved, however, in some brochs by using wooden ladders between the platforms, even if a hatch was required within the roof to allow someone out. It is human nature to want to get to the top once such a tower has been built, even in cases where there is no particularly good reason to do so!

The greatest density of brochs can be found along the east coast of the South Mainland, where each broch would certainly be visible from its neighbour. These brochs may have formed part of a chain to pass warnings or messages from one to the next. Where he could measure the dimensions of the floors accurately, Noel Fojut found that, with the exception of Mousa, brochs in Shetland were similar in size. He suggests that the brochs were all built within a relatively short period of time, under the guidance of one master broch builder; they must have been built in societies where a spirit of co-operation existed.

There are far fewer brochs along the west coast of the South Mainland. In places the cliffs are almost sheer, with few pockets of cultivable land, but elsewhere the coast also includes rich agricultural land; Culswick dominates a considerable seascape on the West Side. It is unlikely that we have a full picture of broch distribution, as more are slowly being found. In 1975 road construction (undertaken as a result of upgrading the airport) uncovered the edge of a broch at Old Scatness (see **colour plate 15**). As we have seen, in 1989, house building at Upper Scalloway led to the discovery of another. Other brochs may have been robbed of stone in order to build later structures.

Some of the brochs seem to have operated in pairs. The broch on the island of Mousa stands opposite the Broch of Burraland on the Mainland, and the pair are well placed to guard the sound between them. Noss Sound, which lies between the islands of Noss and Bressay, is guarded by a broch on the Bressay side. The sound is very narrow, so perhaps one broch was sufficient, but there is a suspiciously broch-sized mound on the Noss side, which is today surmounted by the house at Gungstie. Such brochs may therefore have guarded the sea passages between the islands and the Mainland. People in boats would not relish being forced out into the open sea to go around Mousa or Noss. To slip by unnoticed, in the shadow of the broch, would require a brave or a foolhardy seaman, facing unknown hazards from below the waterline as well as danger from attack if spotted from the shore.

We do not know where the threat which faced the broch builders came from. It has been suggested that brochs were built in order to protect the population from Roman slavers, but there is no evidence that the Romans ever reached Shetland. Agricola's fleet visited Orkney in AD 83, and are said to have sighted Thule. It is not clear precisely what they saw, but Fair Isle is the only land visible looking northwards from Orkney. In about 300 BC the Massilean sailor stated that

Thule lay six days' sailing to the north of Britain. Shetlanders lay claim to the name 'Thule', but some scholars think that Iceland or Norway may be more likely candidates.

Broch sites frequently lie on top of earlier remains and, indeed, often continued to be used for centuries after the broch itself had been abandoned. Every broch excavation in Shetland has uncovered remains of other periods, earlier or later. It may simply be because the brochs are situated in some of the best places for settlement: places which had been discovered and used by earlier generations. The supply of stone would have attracted people to settle near ruins. It may also have been easier to continue to work previously cultivated land than to break out new land; this would certainly have been true at Old Scatness, where the Bronze Age settlers had laboriously created a 'plaggen' soil on the sand (see Chapter 3). In repeatedly using the same place for building, the broch builders were avoiding encroachment on cultivable land.

Archaeologists may never discover exactly why the brochs were built; it is impossible to know how people thought 2000 years ago. The biggest clues may lie in the relationship which the brochs had with the sea.

8
A spoke in the wheel

After a few hundred years, the desire or need to live in brochs passed. The well-built towers were too good just to abandon or pull down, and late Iron Age people chose to convert them into other types of houses, often using them as one house amongst a small group of similar houses. Some brochs were turned into 'wheelhouses', so called because they resemble a wheel in plan: the thick outer wall forms the rim, the projecting stone pillars or piers resemble the spokes, and a central fire lies at the hub.

There are four wheelhouses still visible at Jarlshof, one of which is virtually complete. The three which stand on the north-west side of the broch were each constructed slightly differently (**colour plate 8**). One had been built as a circular building which then had piers inserted (**53**). The piers of the other two were bonded into the outer walls; one had alternating rectangular and

53 Wheelhouse at Jarlshof. The piers of this particular wheelhouse are not bonded into the outer wall. (Historic Scotland)

V-shaped piers; the other had piers which were exclusively V-shaped. This may represent a chronological progression, as the builders became increasingly skilled at their craft. The integrated piers would have made the entire structure more stable. In the two houses where the piers were built into the walls, each of the individual rooms (or cells) which the piers created was corbelled (beehive-shaped). The piers were constructed so as to get steadily wider as they got higher, which was no mean feat of engineering. Each course of stone was placed in such a way as to project beyond the one below, creating a domed ceiling over the cell. This minimized the central area of space which was open to the sky. The space itself may have been corbelled, or it may have been covered with a wood or whalebone framework, perhaps supporting additional slabs.

In the Western Isles, wheelhouses seem to have been built into the sand with only their roofs visible above ground level. There is little reason to think that this was the case at Jarlshof. Although before it was excavated the entire site was covered by windblown sand, the wheelhouses seem to have much the same floor level as the broch, and one of them seems to have been entered via an alleyway which ran between the broch courtyard and the wheelhouse. The houses were extremely substantial, suggesting that they stood alone. Skins and woven cloths hung on the walls would have kept them warm inside and repelled draughts (**54**).

Relatively few wheelhouses have come to light so far, if we exclude the structures which were built inside the brochs. (Some brochs, such as Levenwick and Eastshore, have clear evidence of piers inside the broch tower.) A wheelhouse at Robins Brae was identified when a farmer dug a silage clamp into it! Another was uncovered in 1995 during the excavations at Old Scatness. This stands on the shoulders of the broch mound, and appears to be standing

54 Inside a wheelhouse. (Joanna Richards)

on a floor level considerably higher than the broch floor. So far, all these wheelhouses have been situated in the South Mainland, usually in areas where there has been a lot of movement of sand. This does not necessarily mean that sand was essential to building a wheelhouse; it may be that the wheelhouses which survive do so because they were inundated by sand, so preventing later stone robbing.

Brochs into wheelhouses

There seems to be a link between broch reoccupation and wheelhouses. Robins Brae is the only site in Shetland where a wheelhouse appears to have existed completely independently of a broch. There may be a broch close by which has yet to be found; the build-up of blown sand in the area would make this quite possible. All the broch towers excavated in Shetland to date had been reused. This reduces the amount which archaeologists can find out about the original broch dwellers, since much of the tell-tale evidence was swept away by the new builders. Some of the buildings set into brochs are not true wheelhouses but, even so, the broch floor has been disturbed by later building. Thus today what the visitor sees inside the brochs at Clickhimin and Mousa are later buildings. Most archaeologists have been very reluctant to remove these later walls to investigate beneath them, as removal would be a major and dangerous task. At Clickhimin, the later wall is very thick and probably plays an important role in stabilizing the broch tower today. Removing it might bring the entire broch crashing down!

At Upper Scalloway there was little left of the walling and, since it was due to be destroyed by the twentieth-century house builders, the archaeologists found themselves in the unusual position of being able to dismantle the inner walls without encountering the usual problems.

After the Upper Scalloway broch was destroyed by fire, a wheelhouse with V-shaped pillars was built into the shell of the broch. The pillars have been dated to the fifth or sixth

centuries AD. Either the wheelhouse was never completed, or it was dismantled later, in order to make room for a second building.

This second building was smaller and, although it incorporated two of the piers from the first building, it stood 0.7–0.8m (approx. 2ft) inside the broch wall. The building was partitioned into 'cells'; two partition walls were of stone, while a third was wooden, and these were ranged around a central fireplace. The roof had been held up by a ring of posts, and when it rained the water must have drained into the space between the house and the broch walls. The doorway to the broch continued to be used as the entrance to the house.

When a third building was constructed inside the broch, the builders placed the skull of an elderly woman between the foundations and the first course of stones. This was probably a dedication, perhaps part of a blessing ceremony for the new house. The woman may have been a revered ancestor of the family about to take up residence. This building is very similar to the one which still exists within Mousa Broch. The later house at Mousa is not concentric with the broch tower, and encloses a small irregular area around a hearth and pit, possibly a cooking pit, which is probably dug through the original broch floor. The area behind the later house wall at Mousa was filled in, creating a stone platform between the wall and the house. The top of this platform may have been a sleeping space. The same pattern seems to have existed at Upper Scalloway, where the central space is less than a quarter of the size of the original broch interior. The platforms would have been needed in order for the inhabitants to find enough space in which to sleep! In many ways this concept is not far removed from the arrangement inside brochs, where the living and sleeping platforms were of wood. At Mousa access to the cells in the broch wall can still be gained from the stone platform; at Clickhimin it completely blocks up one of the cells.

These changes in styles of architecture suggest that whatever the motivation had been to build brochs, times had changed sufficiently for this to be irrelevant. The desire for isolation and for dominance in the landscape seems to have passed. Wood was in increasingly short supply; scrubby woodland was severely reduced, and it is possible that supplies of driftwood were becoming less reliable. This may have dictated the need for a building style where wood was not required in any quantity, unlike in the brochs, where it would have been required for the repair and maintenance of the internal structures. The stone platforms found in some of the later broch structures would have made unsatisfactory substitutes for wooden storeys, as they would not have enlarged the amount of living space beyond that of the floor area. The insides of the wheelhouses would have been impressive, however, and there is no suggestion that the population was any the poorer at this time: quite the reverse.

Wheelhouse dwellers

The apparent affluence of the wheelhouse dwellers may be a reflection of more settled times. The quantity of jewellery which they had was far greater than that which their predecessors left behind, and the local population was able to make objects in bronze, silver and gold as well as in iron and copper. The new black burnished style of pottery was far more elegant than the earlier, more functional pottery (55). Some of the pins are more decorative than functional; bone pins were still used for more utilitarian purposes. Double-sided combs began to be used at Upper Scalloway. The gaming pieces from this period

55 Black burnished ware, reconstructed using actual fragments found at Jarlshof. (RCAHMS)

include conical counters, two of which (one from Upper Scalloway, the other a chance find from Mail) are described as 'chessmen' and resemble monks (**colour plate 9**)

Fish was becoming more important in the diet of Upper Scalloway's Late Iron Age population. The fish they ate were larger, and included cod and saithe; people must have been going further off-shore to catch them. There was an increase in the numbers of pigs being butchered, and cattle were eaten in greater quantities than sheep, which were kept primarily for wool and perhaps for milk. Pork and fish were considered to be high-status foods in the medieval period, so it would appear that the living was good for the people of Upper Scalloway.

9
Priests and painted people?

Who were the Picts?

The name 'picti', meaning 'painted ones', was
first used by a Roman writer in AD 297, in a
letter addressed to the Caesar Constantius, in
order to describe the people who raided Roman
Britain along its northern frontier (56). The
people so described appear to have been an
amalgamation of tribes known to have existed
north of the Forth. In earlier times the Picts
may or may not have painted their bodies in
preparation for war, but some of them, at least,
had artistic temperaments, and it is their art
which has gained them popularity today. This
art of carving symbols (first on to wood and
then on to stone) and later carving cross-slabs
did not become established until the sixth
century AD. As a result, 'the Picts' are not
distinguishable in the archaeological record
before that. By the late seventh century a Pictish
king called Bridei was visited at his court by
Columba. Adomnán records that when this
visit took place there was also a regional king
(or a representative of the Pictish king) from
Orkney present. Although we have a very
limited picture of the period from the
archaeological record, by the sixth century
Shetland was very much part of the mainstream
of Pictish politics and life.

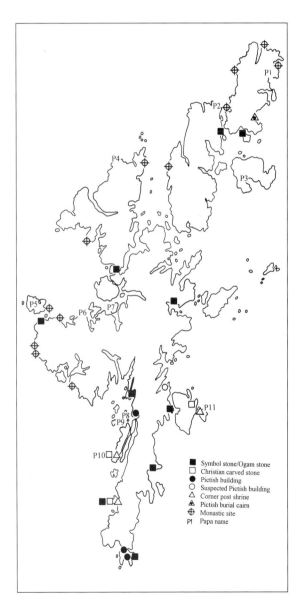

56 Pictish Shetland. Papa names: 1 Papil. 2 Papil.
3 Papil Water. 4 Papa Skerry. 5 Papa Stour.
6 Papa Geo. 7 Papa Little. 8 Papa Skerry. 9 Papa.
10 Papil. 11 Papil Geo. (Anna Purdy)

Legend:
- ■ Symbol stone/Ogam stone
- □ Christian carved stone
- ● Pictish building
- ○ Suspected Pictish building
- △ Corner post shrine
- ▲ Pictish burial cairn
- ⊕ Monastic site
- P1 Papa name

Most Pictish art is religious in character, and it is clear that Christianity reached Shetland at this time. In trying to identify the Picts, however, we are not looking for large groups of incomers, even if the monks and priests were mainly newcomers to Shetland. Although Shetland became part of the Pictish kingdom politically, it is hard to identify what this meant to the ordinary person in practical terms. What did come into Shetland was a set of ready formed ideas and values, together with an associated art style, which is called 'Pictish' in the same way as we term another set of beliefs and art styles 'Renaissance'. Essentially the Shetland Picts were the descendants of the people who had already lived there for generations.

The appearance of Pictish art from the sixth century onwards coincides with the appearance of a distinctive type of building construction (with only one earlier Shetland example, found at Kebister) and with distinctive objects found in association with the houses which are all classified as being 'Pictish'.

Painted pebbles

One of the most characteristic types of objects which Picts in the north of Scotland possessed was 'painted pebbles' (57). To date, only twenty-six have been found, all of them from Caithness, Orkney and Shetland. The rounded painted pebbles vary in size, the smallest being

about 42mm (just over 1.5in) in diameter. The longest known pebble, found at Upper Scalloway, was 78mm (3in) long, but it was broken and may originally have been as much as 90mm (3.5in) long.

The biggest collection of painted pebbles from any one place is the group of five from Upper Scalloway. The Scalloway stones are all of white quartzite painted with solid dots and S-scrolls. The dots are common to most of the pebbles, but the S-scrolls appear to be unique to those found at Upper Scalloway. The S-scroll motive is found elsewhere in Pictish Shetland: a rectangular slate fragment from Jarlshof had a cross on it with expanded terminals and small S-scrolls on the arms; a corner-post from St Ninian's Isle was also decorated with an S-scroll. The painted pebbles therefore would seem to have an association with Christian beliefs, and possibly Irish connections too.

As yet, no one has managed to identify the substance with which the stones were painted. The browny-black stains are resistant to being washed or scrubbed. Some of the dots on the Scalloway stones are fainter than others, so it is possible that either repeated handling in antiquity or weathering over a millennium has had some corrosive effect.

We are no wiser about what the stones were used for. Quartzite may have held some mystical or religious significance for the Picts. The only Pictish burial cairn to be found in Shetland (at the Easting, Sandwick in Unst) was rectangular, outlined with upright stone slabs and covered with quartzite pebbles inside. Perhaps this represents a throwback to Neolithic times when groups of fist-sized quartzite pebbles were placed on at least some of the chambered tombs (for example, at Coppister in Yell). The stones may have been considered valuable, or simply decorative, or they may have represented lucky charms or amulets; Celtic Christianity placed a high value on the natural world, unlike the ultimately more successful Roman Church. Alternatively, the painted pebbles may have been gaming

57 A painted pebble from Jarlshof. (RCAHMS)

pieces, of a somewhat different nature to the smaller 'chessmen' and counters. At present we can only speculate.

Curious symbols

The Picts used about fifty distinctive symbols which they incised (or scratched) on to undressed stones, silver jewellery and perhaps less durable objects as well. Examples of these symbols on stones can be found appearing simultaneously throughout the Pictish kingdom, from Shetland to Fife. Although the symbols are individual to Pictland, the style of art is heavily influenced by mainstream Iron Age art styles in Europe (La Tène) and the Mediterranean. Sometimes the symbols occur alone; in other cases, several symbols are carved on to a single stone, and during the late seventh and early eighth centuries, they were carved alongside Christian iconography. We cannot be certain what purpose the stones served, but the inscriptions seem to include personal names. The stones may have been territorial markers, or memorial stones, or to commemorate political or marriage alliances. Indeed, they may have served all three of these purposes.

There are two classic symbol stones from Shetland (**58**). One, now lost, from Sandness was incised with a rectangle, a mirror and a horseshoe. The other, from Jarlshof, depicted a double disc and Z-rod. The Islesburgh eagle may have been a third symbol stone, or, alternatively, it may have been a Christian representation of the eagle of St John the Evangelist.

Solitary figures carved on to stone seem to have been rather more complex symbols, but probably served the same purpose. The animal-headed figure found at Mail, Cunningsburgh, in 1992 falls into this category (**59**). The figure has a well-executed face (perhaps a mask), but the work on the body is out of proportion and more crude. He (or she, although the figure appears to have a beard) carries an axe over the right shoulder and grips a staff in the left hand. The artist disregarded the flaw across the face

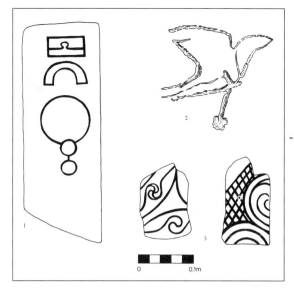

58 Symbol stones: 1 Sandness Stone (rectangle, horse shoe and mirror). 2 Islesburgh eagle. 3 Fragment from Jarlshof. (Anna Purdy)

of the stone, and the figure is not carved in the centre. It may have been a practice piece, but there is some indication that the bottom of the stone was deliberately broken from a larger slab after the figure had been carved. This could explain the strange positioning of the figure, squashed down towards the bottom of the stone as it remains today. The reverse side of the stone may also have been carved, but centuries of weathering have caused layers of stone to split off from that face, taking with them any carving. On the other hand, perhaps that face was never carved because the artist knew it to be less stable. The Mail Stone, as it is known, probably dates to the early seventh century.

Several stone fragments which have Pictish carvings on them but are not, strictly speaking, symbol stones have been discovered in places as diverse as Lerwick, Uyea (North Mainland), Whiteness (Central Mainland), Jarlshof (South Mainland) and South Garth (Yell). These stones are patterned with designs which include spirals, hatchings and zigzags. Like the true symbols, these also date to the seventh–ninth centuries AD.

59 Mail figure. (Val Turner)

A mysterious language?

Pictish society was the first literate society in
Shetland, although literacy was probably
restricted to the upper classes. Written Pictish,
known as ogam script, was written with a series
of strokes which cross a central line. As far as
we know, only twenty-eight ogam inscriptions
still exist from throughout the Pictish kingdom,
ten of which have been found in Shetland, a
remarkable total. The inscriptions are carved on
to stones and date from the eighth and ninth
centuries. Four of the inscriptions come from
Mail, Cunningsburgh, and one of them has part
of a Pictish design on the back. Some of the
other inscriptions occur alongside Christian
carvings; the Bressay Stone, for example, has an
ogam inscription along one edge.

The Pictish language has not yet been
translated successfully. This is largely because
until recently scholars have believed that the
language was pre-Indo-European. Recently,
Katherine Forsyth has argued that this is not
the case, and this makes the possibilities of
translating it more achievable. The Picts
adopted the alphabet from the Irish, probably
in response to Roman literacy, then added their
own letters to the Irish script. The difficulties of
the translators are compounded by the fact that
only 50 per cent of the ogam stones are
sufficiently well preserved to be read; even
those which are well preserved include cracks
and abrasions which make it hard to be certain
which letter they represent.

Once a translator succeeds in reading the
ogams correctly, the problem of interpreting
them follows. A few words are identifiable
because they have Gaelic, Irish or Old Norse
roots. The sentence on the Bressay Stone
contains the words 'meqq' (son), 'crroscc'
(cross) and 'dattrr' (daughter). The word
'meqq' was also written on a slab found at St
Ninian's Isle, and the Lunnasting Stone (**60**)
includes the Pictish name 'Nechton'. The
words on both the Bressay and the Lunnasting
Stones are separated by two dots which look
like a colon, a common technique in Norse

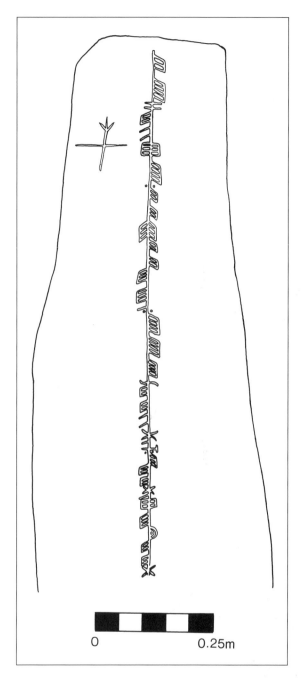

60 Lunnasting Stone. (Anna Purdy)

runic writing. This mixture of cultures suggests
that ogam was far from being pure Pictish, but
reflected the fact that the Picts had close, co-
operative contact with Ireland and (by the
ninth century, in Shetland at least)
Scandinavia.

The 'papar'

When the Vikings settled in Shetland they quickly adopted Christian practices, and continued to use sites which already had a local sacred importance. From the beginning, they seem to have respected communities of monks or priests, the 'papar'. Place-names which include the element 'Papa' are not uncommon in Shetland and seem to reflect the areas where the Vikings first encountered religious enclaves. Papa Stour means 'the big island of the priests'; Papil Geo, situated close to an early Christian cemetery, on the island of Noss, is 'the inlet of the priests'. Since there are better landing sites closer to the cemetery, there may be more to this name still to be unravelled. Papil, on the island of Burra, is a site where cross-slabs and the remains of at least two corner-post shrines have been found, together with what may be the foundations of an early Christian chapel.

Cross-slabs

A cross-slab from Papil, Burra (**61 (a)**), dated to the end of the eighth century AD, is carved in low relief on one side. The slab has a circular cross-head carved on it, and on each side of the cross-shaft, facing each other across the stone, there is a pair of monks. All four monks carry crooks, and one of each pair carries a book satchel; it is clear that at least some of the monks could read. Below this scene is a lion, which bears a close resemblance to the lion of St Mark illustrated in the earlier *Book of Durrow*. Incised at the bottom of the stone (and possibly added at a later date) are two figures with bird beaks and legs. The birds peck at a human skull between them. The figures carry axes over their shoulders in the same way as the Mail figure does (there may once have been more of the central figure, but the stone is damaged at this point). The bird scene has been interpreted as representing the temptation of St Anthony, with two women disguised as birds whispering in his ears!

A similar stone was found in the island of Bressay (**61 (b) and (c)**). Although more crudely carved than the cross-slab from Papil, the

61 (a) Papil stone

(b) and (c) Front and back of the Bressay Stone. (Anna Purdy)

0   0.25m

interlace around the two cross-heads (one on each side of the stone) is more elaborate. There are two monks with satchels on each face of the slab. On the finer face of the stone there is a pony-riding monk between the pair on that side. There are two beasts on either face, three of the four having a similar stance to the Papil lion. An additional pair of beasts appear to be devouring a man at the top of the finer side!

The authentication and dating of a Pictish stone involves considerable detective work. In the case of the Bressay Stone, the verdict of R. B. K. Stevenson is that the finer side may have been carved in the first half of the ninth century, but the rougher side may have been carved as much as a century later. Whoever carved it must have been familiar with the Papil cross-slab, which was presumably still standing when the Bressay Stone was worked.

Saints and holymen

In the sixth century AD British people began the practice of venerating saints and holymen by placing their bones in shrines. At first the shrines were made of wood (as were the early cross-slabs), but gradually stone became more commonly used. When Christianity came to Shetland, naturally the practice of using stone shrines was also adopted. The remains of stone shrines have been found at three sites in Shetland: St Ninian's, Papil and Noss (**62**).

When a saint, missionary or holyman was first buried, he (or she?) was buried in the ground like everyone else, then at a later date the grave was opened and the body removed, by which time it would normally have reduced to bones. Usually, the skull together with some of the larger bones survived to be collected and placed in the shrine. Shrines usually had a lid which the worshippers could remove so that they could see and touch the bones.

A corner-post shrine would normally have four rectangular posts, each of which had long grooves (about 2.5cm (1in) deep and 2.5cm (1in) wide) on two adjacent faces. The grooves stopped short of the ends of each post where

62 Corner-post shrine exploded using the Monk Stone from Papil as one side. (Anna Purdy)

their bases were secured into the ground. The side slabs of the shrine were flat, and the vertical edges of each panel were thinned and the corners trimmed in order to produce 'tongues' which slotted into the grooves in the corner-posts. Once the shrine was fitted together with the bases of the posts secured into the ground, it would have been rigid. If there was a lid, it fitted on to the top of the shrine and rested on the side slabs, below the tops of the posts. Some of the St Ninian's corner-posts had knobs carved on their tops; others had debased dolphins incised on them, which would place at least one of the shrines in the early ninth century.

Uniquely, one of the long sides of one of the Papil shrines was carved in relief with a procession of five monks, one of whom is riding a pony, journeying over spirals (the sea?) towards a cross set on a rectangular base. It is very similar in style to the Papil cross-slab, and probably also dates to the late eighth century. The maximum size of any of the single shrines which have been discovered is about 1m by 0.5m (3ft by 1ft 6in). As the long bones (arms and legs) were unlikely to measure any more than 0.55m (20in), the shrines were plenty big enough to contain even a fairly complete skeleton.

Double shrines had two additional central posts; these had long grooves on three faces to hold two lateral slabs and a central partition. The remains of at least two double shrines were found at St Ninian's, and another was discovered at Papil. When the Papil shrine was first found, one of the central posts was still standing, together with the three side slabs which it supported. There was also a skull at the foot of the post: unfortunately, we don't know whose!

St Ninian's Isle

St Ninian's Isle is situated just off the south-west coast of Shetland, linked to the Mainland by a sand bar, or tombolo. The chapel site there was excavated during the 1950s, and it appears that

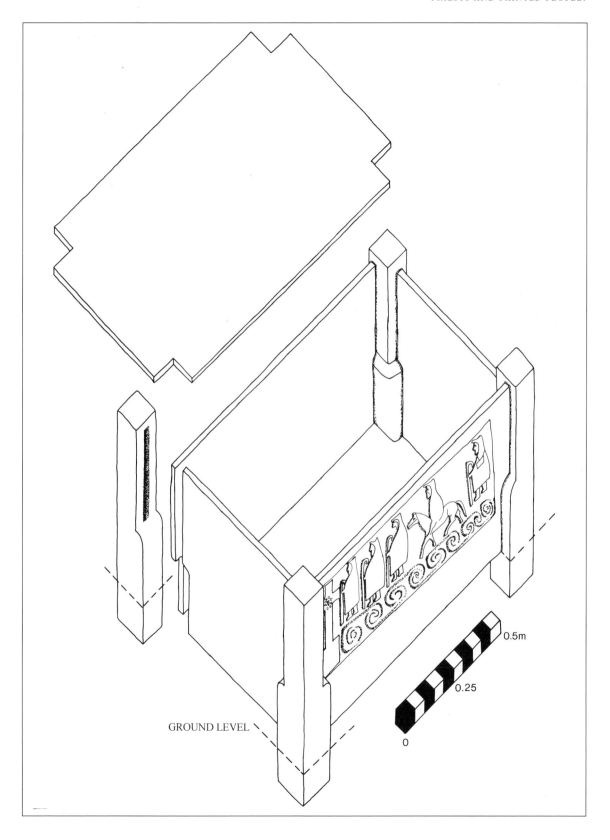

GROUND LEVEL

0.5m

0.25

0

the site was used for burial from the pre-Christian Iron Age, continuing in use during the Pictish Iron Age and on through the Christian Norse period, right up to the last known burial in about 1840 (**colour plate 10**).

The pre-Christian Iron Age burials were in short slab cists. Six were found, one still containing the bones of an adult and a child. The adult (thought to be a woman) lay on her side, with her knees drawn up to her chest. In time, burial in short cists was replaced by the burial of extended bodies in long cists. The long cists were the first Christian burials on the site, and the graves (which are contemporary with the shrines) were aligned in the same direction as the Pictish chapel which was subsequently built on the site. This chapel was later replaced with a slightly bigger chapel, which was further enlarged during the eleventh or twelfth centuries, when a number of chapels were built in Shetland. The island was finally abandoned as a chapel site in 1744.

Five carved steatite stones and a hog-back grave cover were found during the St Ninian's Isle excavation. Four of the stones had crosses carved on to them, and the fifth was shaped into a cross. These were probably all grave markers and probably Norse rather than Pictish, evidence of the continuing use of the site. The plain steatite hog-back grave cover, about 1.25m (4ft) long, was also Norse.

The furthest-travelled of the finds from St Ninian's was a tiny fragment of *porfido verde antico* (mottled, but predominantly green, marble), a polished stone from southern Greece. It may originally have been inset into a shrine. Similar fragments have been found during excavations at Kebister, near Lerwick, and at the monastery at Whithorn, in Galloway, the home of Ninian in the fifth century. Archaeologists have tended to believe that it was the eleventh–twelfth-century chapel which was dedicated to St Ninian, superseding an earlier, Celtic, dedication. If, however, the Ninian dedication is earlier, it would suggest that Shetland had contact with the mainstream European Roman Church at a far earlier date.

Treasure!

Around AD 800, danger threatened the south-west coast of Shetland. Chapels have long been places of refuge in troubled times, and this must have prompted someone to gather up the family silver (twenty-eight items in all), together with the jaw-bone of a porpoise (a lucky charm, perhaps?), and place it in a larchwood box. They buried the box beneath the floor of the chapel on St Ninian's Isle and covered it with a slab which had a cross carved on it. The treasure was kept safely enough, but presumably the danger overtook the owners, as they never returned to recover it. It lay undisturbed until the excavations in 1958 (**colour plate 11**) (Chapter 1). The treasure may have been hidden in response to Viking raids, although, at present, it is an isolated example of panic.

There is no reason to think that the silver was ecclesiastical. The collection of pieces, in several different styles, with artistic parallels with Ireland, Northumbria and southern England as well as Pictland, included seven shallow drinking bowls, a hanging bowl (fashionable in the seventh century, although more usually made of bronze), sword fittings (including a chape inscribed in Latin on both sides), three cones (perhaps button fastenings) and eleven penannular brooches in a range of sizes.

The richness of the treasure demonstrates that some of the Shetland Picts owned considerable wealth. The St Ninian's Isle Treasure could not have been an isolated example, otherwise the chances are that its loss would have been known and the treasure recovered from its relatively predictable hiding place.

Hermits

Along some of Shetland's more rugged shores there are high off-shore stacks (detached cliffs). These are formed in places where cliffs have become detached from the mainland as a result of erosion and the collapse of land bridges, creating islets which are now virtually inaccessible by either land or sea. There are also many headlands accessible only via high knife-edge ridges which will themselves eventually fall into the sea. Although more than 1000 years of coastal erosion have made these locations more inaccessible than they once were, these places were always remote, hard to reach and at the mercy of the weather. It is difficult to believe that anyone would have chosen to build, far less live, in such remote and exposed situations, and yet that is what they did! There are several such places, particularly on the West Side of Shetland and in the North Isles, where groups of small square or rectangular foundations, some as small as 2m by 3m (6ft by 10ft), were built in turf or stone. The buildings vary in size and number, but their overall shape and layout, together with their situations, suggest that these sites all served much the same function. (A structure built in a similar situation at Fethaland, Northmavine, *c.* AD 1900, is recorded by the Royal Commission as being built by a man 'who was generally agreed to be mad'.) The larger sites seem to have been monasteries or communal retreats; the single sites are presumably hermitages, or places for individual retreat. If contemporary, these monastic communities must have served a very different purpose from the farms of the missionary 'papar' who settled in the middle of fertile areas and worked with the local communities.

In several cases, the ground of the settlement slopes away from the mainland, down to the open sea. Some of the 'islets' have walls or banks across the landward end of the settlement. As a result, the buildings would have been fairly well hidden from the land. The Kame of Isbister (Northmavine) and the Birrier of West Sandwick (Yell) (**colour plate 12**) face each other across the sea of Yell Sound, the land on each sloping towards the other. Raymond Lamb, whose intrepid study of the sites involved swimming out to some of them carrying ranging rods and equipment, and on whose invaluable information we rely, observed nineteen buildings at the Kame of Isbister and thirteen on the Birrier. Twenty-three buildings were recorded on the Kame by a theology student in

the 1870s, when the island was more easily accessible. The landward approach to both sites is across peat bog, of little practical use to the inhabitants except as fuel.

In addition to these communal sites, a handful of off-shore pillars of rock had room for just one rectangular building in the middle, with an encircling wall around the summit. Two such stacks in Burri Geo at Culswick fit the same general description which Bede gave of Cuthbert's hermitage in the Farne Islands.

It is generally supposed that the stack dwellers lived on sea-birds; as a long-term diet this would have led to scurvy. Fresh water must also have presented a problem: there would be little usable water in the peat bogs and, unless spring water was available on the stack-tops, the residents would have been forced to collect rain water. The austerity imposed on the stack-top communities by the restricted diet, potentially vicious weather and general life-style may indicate that the monasteries were occupied seasonally, perhaps by a fluid population of 'papar' going into retreat. However, all the community-based religious centres seem to be a long distance from the coastal monastic sites, and it is possible that the two types of site represent quite separate Christian traditions. If the sites were occupied permanently, there must have been an associated community elsewhere which helped to supply them with food. The easiest way to transport goods would have been by sea, but most of the monasteries are at some distance from suitable bays or harbours and the monks may still have had to walk for an hour or more over peat moorland in order to fetch supplies. Alternatively, people may have risked the dangers of sailing to the bottom of the cliffs in small boats, and may have sent supplies up by means of baskets lowered from above on heather or straw ropes.

Apart from an inconclusive trench dug at the Kame of Isbister in 1870, the positions of these sites have ensured that they escape the trowel of the archaeologist. There are, however, a few similar stack-top sites in Orkney, in the north of

Scotland, and in Ireland. At one of these sites, at Dinnacair near Stonehaven, Pictish stones have been found. It is possible, however, that this site was originally a promontory fort, and so may not indicate the date and function of the monastic sites. Raymond Lamb has recently suggested that these sites are later than archaeologists have hitherto thought, and that they may in fact have been inhabited during the tenth–eleventh centuries AD, when the extremity of this way of life would have been in keeping with the then prevalent ideals of monasticism. Until such time as an archaeologist is brave enough, or rash enough, to excavate one of these sites, we will remain uncertain.

A Pictish powerbase?

Mail lies in the south of Cunningsburgh, on the south-east coast of Mainland Shetland. The Norse name Cunningsburgh has been translated as 'the king's broch' or 'the king's fortress'. There are at least three broch sites in the immediate vicinity, and one of these lies just off-shore from (and was once attached to) the point of Mail. The point protects a sandy bay, sheltered by the mainland to the north and west and, to some extent, to the south as well. The land to the north of Mail is flat and fertile, whilst that to the south-west rises to form hills which include the steatite outcrops along Catpund Burn (see page 109–111). We have already seen that steatite was known to be a valuable commodity as early as Neolithic times, when it was used for tempering pottery. It was easy to crush and to carve, and by the Bronze Age, blocks of the stone were occasionally used to carve urns, which seem to have been used primarily as cremation vessels. There are a few examples of Iron Age vessels from Upper Scalloway, but the use of steatite was to reach its zenith in the Viking and Norse periods. Catpund, the largest (although not the only) source of Shetland steatite, would have been a valuable place to control. Although the Catpund quarries were doubtless well used during the Pictish period, their visible remains appear to be Viking and Norse in date.

Mail graveyard, situated on the point, is where the 'Mail Stone' was found. Three ogam stones, three rune stones and another 'Pictish stone' were also found there. There are local references to other 'scratchet stanes' (carved stones), now lost, having been found in the graveyard, and hearths have allegedly been uncovered in the course of grave-digging in the area.

As with everything in the Pictish period, the evidence for a Shetland centre of Pictish power is shadowy. Nevertheless, the structure of Pictland was hierarchical, and it is not unreasonable to assume that there might have been a Pictish powerbase to be found in Shetland. On the basis of the evidence which we do have, Mail is a possible location for such a powerbase and would certainly repay investigation.

Where did people live?

The only distinctive Pictish buildings discovered to date in Shetland have been found in and around the ruins of brochs. Those excavated at Jarlshof, Upper Scalloway and Old Scatness are similar in shape to buildings found near the broch of Gurness and at Buckquoy (where there was no broch) in Orkney. The Shetland buildings were small and insubstantial and would probably never have been found if the brochs had not attracted archaeologists to work on the site. There must be many more examples awaiting discovery, if only archaeologists knew where to look. If this type of Pictish building were accidentally uncovered by gardeners or builders, it is unlikely that it would be recognized, as the remains are so slight and easily destroyed. Indeed, the series of hearths reported by grave-diggers at Mail may once have been inside Pictish buildings (63).

Some of the Pictish buildings were built while the wheelhouses were still in use. At least some of the Pictish buildings are a different shape from all the prehistoric houses which preceded them. They consist of a series of curvilinear 'cells', attached to one another either in a figure-of-eight shape or linked to one another by a short passageway.

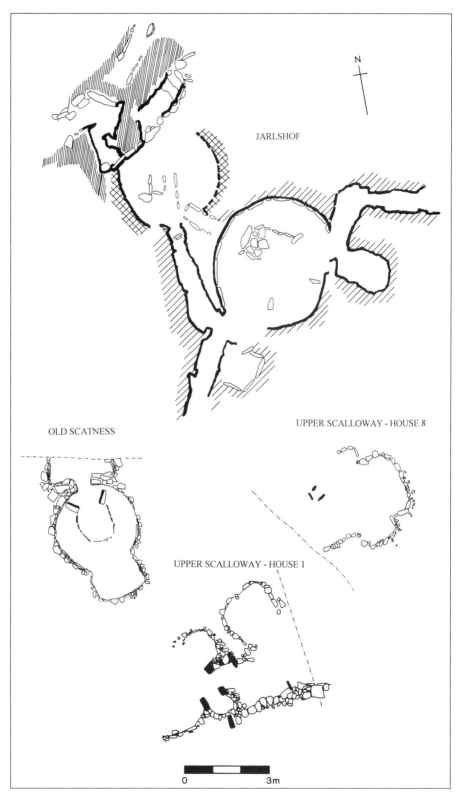

63 Pictish building plans (after Hamilton, Bond and Sharples). (Anna Purdy)

The bottom course of stones in the walls consisted of small vertical uprights which supported courses of small stones above. These walls revetted an outer structure; the buildings were 'semi-subterranean', built either into blown sand or into the debris of earlier settlement (for example, Upper Scalloway) or clad in thick layers of earth or turf. Shetland dry-stone dykers have suggested that, in stark contrast to the brochs, the revetting stone walls of a cellular building could have been built in a day.

Some cells in the buildings contained a central hearth, outlined by a line of small stones set on edge. 'Hut 2' at Jarlshof is considerably larger than the others and contained a bench of sand and turf, with a stone facing, beside the central hearth. Although styled a 'hut' by the excavator, it could easily have been a dwelling house. This building also contained the foundations of three possible piers which may have supported the roof. The other buildings had no visible means of roof support, although they would have been fairly easy to roof by anchoring the supporting frame into the external cladding of turf, soil or rubble.

There is one exception to the general rule of cellular buildings being sixth-century in date; a house excavated at Kebister was shown by radiocarbon dating to have gone out of use before AD 400. The Kebister house was free-standing and earth-clad, and not dug into the ground. As one would expect from the early date, the house contained both broch and wheelhouse types of pottery, but there were no distinctively Pictish objects. Objects which archaeologists term 'Pictish' have only been identified from the sixth century and later but, as we saw earlier, the Romans first identified people whom they called 'Picts' in the late third century. Perhaps the seeds of a trend which was to develop into what archaeologists today describe as 'Pictish' had reached Kebister as early as the fourth century AD.

The house at Kebister stood alongside earlier, but still occupied, Iron Age houses in the same way that the cellular houses at Upper Scalloway were used at the same time that the broch was being reoccupied. We need to find more cellular houses in Shetland before we can be precise about how Kebister fits into the sequence, but since three of the four 'Pictish house' sites have been found during the last ten years, we can confidently expect more to appear.

The material culture of the Picts hardly suggests a community on the bread-line, but it seems strange that we have only scrappy remains of their buildings. The Upper Scalloway and Old Scatness buildings may have been workshops, and not the main dwelling houses at all. They are so small that people sleeping in them would have been in severe danger of rolling into the fire. Fragments of crucibles were found on the floor at both, and at Old Scatness minute fragments of hammerscale (ironworking residue) and slag ash have been identified: evidence that metalworking took place there. The building at Old Scatness contained a lot of charred grain (**64**). Since wood was in short supply, charred grain would have made a good source of fine-grained charcoal. If the buildings were smithies, this might explain why they were dark and almost subterranean; darkness would have assisted the smith to see subtle, but crucial, changes of colour in the metal as it was heated. In this case, we might expect to find the remains of dwellings close by.

The main Pictish houses may have been built of a less durable material, such as timber or turf. As in previous centuries, if such buildings were not constructed close to stone-built sites they would be difficult, if not impossible, to find today. Scientific techniques are continually extending the boundaries of archaeological work, however, and in time the prospect of making discoveries may alter. By the sixth century AD, most of the native woodland had long been destroyed and driftwood, the main source of timber, would have been highly prized. To live in a timber house under such circumstances would have been a sign of real affluence.

In mainland Britain, timber structures are often identified through 'crop marks' observed

64 Building a Pictish smithy (based on remains found at Old Scatness). (Joanna Richards)

by aerial photography. When fields of grain are in the process of ripening, the amount of moisture in the soil is critical. In a dry summer, the roots of the crops have to penetrate more deeply in order to find water. If a timber post has rotted, or if there is a pit where there had once been a post (a post-hole), the soil in that particular area retains slightly more moisture than that around it, and the ears of grain above it ripen fractionally faster than the rest of the field. If there are stones, perhaps the remains of a wall, buried within the field, the crops above develop more slowly. An archaeologist in the air at the crucial moment (which may last for as little as a few hours) can see the change from green to yellow as the crops ripen differentially. Unfortunately, so little grain is grown in Shetland, and the summers are usually so wet, that aerial photography for crop marks is not as valuable as it is elsewhere. Until archaeological

techniques have been developed further, it will remain extremely difficult to locate timber buildings of any period in Shetland.

Another reason why late Iron Age buildings are so difficult to find may be associated with their location. If Pictish houses were built in the best locations, on or close to good arable land, with fresh water close by and ready access to the sea, the chances are that the site would have been built on repeatedly through time. The Vikings would have wanted the best land when they arrived, and as there is no reason to assume that they walked into an empty landscape, Viking houses must frequently have been built over Pictish ones, and would, in turn, have developed into the centres of crofting communities. This is what happened at Jarlshof where, although sandblow obscured the density of settlement from succeeding generations, the site was used during a 4000-year period. Close by, the site at Old Scatness was used repeatedly for building from at least the Iron Age, and possibly earlier, even into the nineteenth century.

The place-name element 'petta' is thought to refer to a place where the Norse settlers found, or expected to find, Picts. All the places which have 'petta' elements (for example, Petta Water, Pettadale) are in fairly remote inland valleys. These may have been places which would have been the last to have been taken over or influenced by the Viking incomers, and the name probably indicates some of the last outposts of purely Pictish society.

It is even possible that the Vikings came in and replaced the Picts at Jarlshof, where 'Hut 2' was replaced by a rectangular building. The rectangular shape was a radical departure from the curved buildings of prehistoric Shetland, but the builders were still using the Pictish style: a basal course of stones supporting a horizontal stone revetment. The finds from this building include typically Viking-style objects such as steatite loom weights, whorls and vessels, together with stone discs and pounders, which were common in Pictish times.

Once the Pictish smithy at Old Scatness was abandoned, it was levelled off and infilled with stone which was mixed up with Norse material. A silver Anglo-Saxon coin, minted between AD 930 and 970, was found in the same phase. Further excavation might show whether the site was abandoned or whether the incomers took it by force. At Underhoull, in Unst, in the north of Shetland there are traces of a long-lived house, built during the broch period, underneath a Norse house. Archaeologists carrying out further work on this island may also help to flesh out our knowledge of what became of the Picts when the Vikings arrived.

10
A haven for Vikings

Why did the Vikings come to Shetland?
The Vikings began to raid in Britain around AD 790 and almost certainly rested and raided in Shetland *en route*. Several factors motivated them to leave Scandinavia in search of pastures new. Good farmland was limited in the homelands and the population was increasing. Land was subdivided equally between siblings on inheritance, which led to the land units becoming ever smaller, and eventually unviable, for farming. Feuds between several of the leading families were doubtless exacerbated by the economic situation. The Vikings initially set out to raid and return to their homelands with whatever wealth they could acquire. Others became more interested in finding new land to farm and settle and, in the case of the upper classes, to rule.

During the preceding two centuries the climate had gradually improved, and the seas were becoming less treacherous. Meanwhile, the Vikings had developed sea-going clinker-built boats, the sides of which were constructed of overlapping planks (strakes) held together by iron rivets and caulked with animal hair. These 'pirate ships' were built to be light, strong, slender and flexible; they had tapering prows and sterns, and hulls which were reinforced across the width (**65**). The masts could be raised or lowered, so that the Vikings could either take full advantage of the wind or be less conspicuous when hiding in voes or making surprise attacks. The Vikings also had high-sided, wide cargo ships for serious

trade, and these would doubtless have been used when they needed to import wood and livestock in order to set themselves up in Shetland with a house and farm.

Viking seamen had two major advantages over earlier adventurers: the keel and the sun-bearing compass, which gave them increased control over where they went. Now they could steer their ships from the stern, and travel was no longer dependent on being able to see the sun; as long as the day was bright enough to create a shadow, the Vikings could stay on course.

Taking all these circumstances together, Viking society was ripe for adventure and emigration. For the Vikings leaving Northern and Western Norway, Shetland would have been the first landfall. It would have looked very familiar to them: a land where tongues of sea flowed inland (although the voes of Shetland are far shorter and shallower than the Norwegian fjords) and where hills (rather than mountains) rose behind the coastal plain. Shetland would have been similar to home, but softer – a promised land!

The houses of the earliest Viking settlers have been neither positively identified nor excavated, but the newcomers may have begun to settle fairly soon after the raids began.

The Viking impact
Perhaps the most sweeping effect of Viking settlement in Shetland was a complete alteration of the language. The vast majority of Shetland

65 This etching, probably drawn by a Pict living at Jarlshof, is thought to represent the dragon prow of a Viking ship. (Historic Scotland)

place-names have Norse origins, and the modern Shetland dialect contains many Norse words. At the end of the nineteenth century the Faroese scholar Jakob Jakobsen identified over 10,000 Norse words in the Shetland dialect. Traditionally, by the end of the ninth century the Norse earldom of Orkney and Shetland is thought to have been established and was ruled by Norwegian earls. The changes to the language, however, could not have been brought about by a new upper class alone. To change the spoken language so completely would have required a very large group of settlers, people who farmed the land and needed names for every corner. Raymond Lamb has argued that the Pictish nobility had little interest in the sea and, when the raiding began, invited opposing groups of Vikings to come to protect the islands.

Viking or Norse?

The terms 'Viking' and 'Norse' can be confusing. The word 'Viking' originally referred to pirates who hid in bays (*vik*) waiting to strike. Today the term is generally used to cover the period of raiding and early settlement, between AD 800 and 1000. In Shetland, the period AD 1000–1500 is usually described as Norse, although some scholars prefer to use the term 'medieval'. During the Norse period the everyday life of the Shetlanders was akin to that of their Scandinavian counterparts: they used similar objects and adhered to the same fashions. Politically, until 1195 Shetland was part of the earldom of Orkney and Shetland; after an uprising in 1194, Shetland was administered directly from Norway (in order to punish the earl). The situation altered in 1469 when Shetland was pawned to Scotland by Christian I, King of Denmark and Norway, in part payment of the dowry of his daughter, Margaret, on her marriage to James III of Scotland; however, Shetland's subsequent history is beyond the scope of this book.

Viking settlement

The Viking settlers probably arrived gradually and intermarried; eventually there were sufficient numbers of them for them to become dominant and absorb the Picts. The incoming population may have respected the 'papar' (priests), who apparently continued to flourish without any discernible break, but the place-name evidence suggests that the Vikings took over most of the best arable land and, on some occasions at least, this might have required a degree of force. The archaeological evidence for this is, however, as elusive as the evidence of Pictish houses.

The evidence for Viking settlement is slight, possibly because many houses may have been built entirely of wood from Norway and have left little trace. The houses discovered so far resemble Late Iron Age houses from Western Norway built in stone and turf, with the use of timber restricted to the inside of the building (**66**). The settlements at Jarlshof and Old

Scatness demonstrate the reuse of sites throughout the Norse period, and this too may have destroyed earlier evidence.

Reports of substantial structures being found during building work on and around crofthouses are slowly increasing the numbers of known Viking and Norse (as well as prehistoric) sites. Some of these foundations have been accompanied by spectacular finds: Gord, Fetlar and North House, Papa Stour have both produced steatite lamps together with other fine and identifiably Norse or Viking objects.

A third factor in the disappearance of Viking sites is undoubtedly their proximity to the sea. The Vikings favoured house sites close to sloping sandy beaches, particularly along more sheltered voes, so that they could pull their boats ashore more easily and because such beaches were usually backed by fertile land. As sea level in Shetland has risen about 1m (3ft)

66 Inside a Viking house. (Joanna Richards)

since then, a lot of gently sloping arable land has gradually disappeared underwater. The two late Norse houses and the Pictish burial cairn excavated on the beach at the Easting, Sandwick, in Unst, demonstrate the destructive power of the sea. Even as excavation at North Sandwick was taking place, the sea was washing over the site at high tide; eventually, it will be washed away.

Jarlshof: a Viking township

Situated in the South Mainland of Shetland, amongst good, flat, fertile land with a sandy bay close by, Jarlshof was first inhabited in the Bronze Age. It is one of the few Viking sites which has been excavated in Shetland (**colour plate 13**). Jarlshof, however, was excavated before radiocarbon dating existed, and so we do not have a precise date for the establishment of the first Viking house. The excavator suggested a ninth-century date for the Viking house, but other archaeologists have placed the date later. The ephemeral remains of the rectangular building above Pictish 'Hut 2' might represent earlier Viking settlement, and there may be earlier remains beneath the Viking house displayed today.

According to the sagas, a Viking who travelled to Iceland chose a site for his farm and then sent home to Norway for the timber to build it. This may have been common practice amongst Viking settlers in Shetland. Initially, an upturned boat would have made an adequate short-term shelter. The general pattern of house building in Viking Shetland was to use stone facings with an earth or rubble core. The buildings were essentially rectangular, although they narrowed at either end, totally different from the prehistoric buildings which had oval external walls. The change in shape was doubtless made because timber was in plentiful supply in Scandinavia and lends itself to rectangular shapes more easily than stone, Shetland's more readily available building material. Indeed, the style of building in Viking Shetland was imported more or less wholesale

from the west coast of Iron Age Norway.

Unusually, the outer wall at Jarlshof seems to have been built of alternate courses of turf and earth. One of the long walls was slightly bowed while the other was straighter, a shape repeated at Underhoull. Inside the house the walls were probably timber-lined. A 'goal-post' frame supported the wooden roof, which was probably covered in turf, held in place with straw on heather ropes (simmons) weighted with stones. The house measured about 22m by 5m (72ft by 16ft) internally, although some of the length may have been lost from the east end because of later rebuilding. A small area at the west end was partitioned off to form a kitchen which had a central hearth for heating stones, and an adjacent oven. The rest of the building was used for both living and working. Benches along each of the long walls would have served as seats by day and beds by night. One hundred and fifty loom weights, which would have been used to weight the warp threads of an upright loom, were found together with spindle whorls; carding, spinning and weaving were probably common activities within the house.

The main farming activities would have been centred on the three associated outhouses, which have been interpreted as a byre, a smithy and a corn-drying room. There was clinker on the floor of the smithy, and the corn-drying room contained an exceptionally large hearth in the centre. Two other suggestions have been put forward for the purpose of this room: that it was either a sauna or a temple. In time this building was replaced by two outhouses.

Some time later the house itself was modified. The east end was demolished and a byre built on, transforming the house into a 'longhouse'. The byre was paved along the centre and the animals were stalled on either side. An entrance was built in the east gable wall, but it appeared to be far too narrow to have admitted a cow. This puzzle was solved when Sandwick South, at the Easting in Unst, was excavated. The remains of the door at Sandwick stood a metre high, and it was equally narrow at the bottom.

As the doorway rose, however, it widened out and was in fact cow-shaped!

Unlike humans, cows could not have tolerated a smoky atmosphere. This created a potential problem in the longhouse. The Vikings may have solved this problem by fitting a roof which curved down in height at the byre end of the building. This shape, combined with the body heat of the animals, would have circulated the air in such a way as to keep the byre end smoke-free. Meanwhile, the body heat of the cattle would have helped to keep the living quarters warmer. The floor of the Jarlshof byre appears to slope towards the middle of the house, possibly an accident of reconstruction. Longhouses are often found aligned downhill, with the byre situated at the lower end to facilitate drainage.

Extra rooms were added to the long walls of the house. This appears to be a common feature of Shetland longhouses, occurring at both houses excavated in Unst: Underhoull and Sandwick South. (Similar outbuildings have also been found attached to Icelandic longhouses.) Each has a drain which leaves the building through a lintelled gap in the wall. The consistent discovery of drains in the Shetland buildings has led some people to suggest that they housed toilets. Given a site with good organic preservation, one day we should be able to demonstrate whether or not this is true.

Eventually the longhouse was abandoned and used as a byre. During the ensuing centuries, a series of replacement houses was built at 90° to the original alignment. These houses were modified over time, but there were never more than two in use at any given period; by the thirteenth century the inhabited houses at Jarlshof had begun to resemble a typical Shetland croft: a complex of house, byre and several ruins.

Viking Unst

Unst is the most northerly island of Shetland, situated at the crossroads of the western Viking migration routes; the first landfall of Vikings travelling from northern and western Norway to Britain. Recent survey in the island has identified the remains of at least thirty farms which may be Viking or Norse. Three of these have been excavated since the 1960s: Underhoull, on the west coast, and two sites at the Easting, Sandwick.

Some of the houses are low-lying and close to modern crofts; others are in less advantageous positions. The house at Belmont, for example, lies in land used today for rough grazing, halfway up a hill.

Trial excavation at a house at Hamar in the centre of the east coast of Unst has revealed an outstanding single-period house, possibly the best-preserved, but as yet unexcavated, Viking house in Scotland. It may have been abandoned relatively quickly on account of the infertile nature of the surrounding land. The house at Hamar is aligned downhill, whereas the eighteenth- and nineteenth-century crofthouses, which often occupied the same sites as the Viking houses, are aligned predominantly along the hill. The theory that the turning of the favoured direction for building through 90° took place during the Norse period may be borne out by Jarlshof and possibly Underhoull, but more work is required in order to be certain.

The main house at Hamar appears to have had benches along the wall, the tops level with the exterior ground level, with the central floor being sunk into the subsoil. The outer walls were thus relatively low and the house would have hugged the ground. This would have afforded the house protection from the elements in a windswept landscape where farms were set at some distance from one another.

The house at Underhoull is situated below a broch, above a sandy beach and on fertile, if wet, land. The house does not seem to have been used for a lengthy period. The excavator suggested a tenth-century date; more recently a tenth–twelfth-century date has been proposed, as a result of a re-examination of the finds. The house is a typical longhouse, measuring 17.7m (58ft) long, with outhouses attached to one long wall and a byre at the east end. This end is slightly higher than the west end, but the whole house is aligned across the slope and so the direction of drainage is likely to be down the hill. A drain built outside the house on the higher side would have helped to protect the building from water running off the hill.

On the other side of the island, a system of sand dunes became destabilized at the turn of the twentieth century. By the 1930s, the remains of three structures and associated Norse finds had been reported from the bay. These structures may have represented three discrete farm units, or have been part of one chronological sequence. The most northerly site was completely eroded by the sea without archaeological investigation; the middle one, known as Sandwick North, is frequently attacked by high tides and has been excavated recently.

Sandwick South is the first Viking or Norse site from Shetland to yield any radiocarbon dates. It was built in the twelfth century, reached its height in the following two centuries, and foundered in the early 1400s. It consisted of a longhouse and associated side structures. The bone preservation on the site was good, providing a more complete picture of the Norse economy than the site at Underhoull had revealed.

Not surprisingly, as a result of the number of farms in Unst as well as its key position in the Viking seaways, Unst is attracting the attention of leading international Viking specialists, and it may not be too long before Unst yields answers to some of the key problems of rural Viking settlement.

Daily life

Viking and Norse farms seem to have continued to be organized along similar lines to their Shetland predecessors. Wool seems to have been a staple, to judge by the numbers of spindle whorls and loom weights found at Jarlshof. The impression of tabby weave cloth on the back of the tortoise-shaped brooch from Dunrossness shows that people were wearing clothes made

from material which was probably homespun. In addition to cattle, sheep and pigs, the Vikings also kept hens and had ponies, which would have been useful as draught animals on the farm as well as for travelling overland. The improved climate would have made harvests more reliable. Although there were fewer querns in the Viking and Norse levels at Jarlshof than there had been in earlier levels, this may have coincided with the introduction of horizontal mills. The larger line-sinkers of the later Norse period at Jarlshof, together with the fish-bone evidence from

67 Bone pins found at Jarlshof. Their heads represent two animals, an axe and a cross. (National Museums of Scotland)

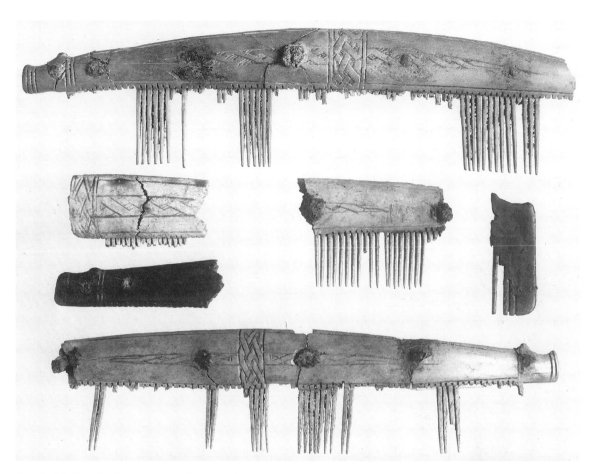

Sandwick South, demonstrate that people were going out fishing in deeper water than previously.

Unlike their predecessors, the Vikings were not very good at making pottery; they preferred to use natural materials such as wood instead. A wooden plate was preserved in a peat bog at Walls, but the lack of trees in Shetland meant that the Vikings needed to look for alternative materials. Bone and antler were commonly used in place of wood. Bone combs have been found on many of the excavated Norse house sites (**68**). The carved teeth were set between two pieces of bone which were held together by rivets and were decorated. Bone was also carved into pins, some of which were decorated with thistles or cross-heads, while others had high-quality animal heads (**67**).

The Jarlshof excavations produced an abundance of metal finds which were not paralleled in Unst, probably because of the corrosive effects of the sea. The smith may have

68 Bone combs from Jarlshof. (National Museums of Scotland)

made most, if not all, the iron objects found on site: sickles, shears, scissors, a large fish-hook (a similar one was also found at Sandwick South) and a knife which had an oak handle. As at Wiltrow (see Chapter 5), the iron smithed at Jarlshof was obtained from bog-ore.

Glass beads and jet jewellery must have been imported, possibly traded in exchange for soapstone, meat or fish. Interestingly, the jet must have originated in Whitby, whether or not it arrived in Shetland through the Viking world.

Viking quarries

The majority of vessels recovered from excavated sites were made from steatite (**69**), which was, in many respects, the ideal substitute for timber; other local stone, for example

69 Steatite (soapstone) vessels found at Jarlshof. The excavator, J. R. C. Hamilton, thought that their rectangular shape dated them to the Norse settlement period. (National Museums of Scotland)

sandstone at Jarlshof and schist in Unst, was used to make the querns and whetstones. Steatite, also known as soapstone, is a soft rock containing a high proportion of talc. The talc content makes it easy to carve or crush: it can even be scratched with a fingernail. It is very fire-resistant and becomes non-porous when it is heated, properties which have led twentieth-century Shetlanders to use it for hearths and firebricks. The Vikings made regular use of steatite in the homelands. The earlier Viking settlers seemed to make small round vessels and vessels with handles, but in the tenth century rectangular vessels were introduced. The Vikings also used flat 'baking plates' and larger round vessels throughout the period. The soft

stone was also used to make the net-sinkers, loom weights, spindle whorls, lamps (which were filled with seal oil and had a floating wick which would have been lit with an iron strike-a-light) and even toys such as miniature millstones (see page 114). The Norse name for steatite was 'kleberg', literally 'loom-weight stone'; in Shetland dialect it is 'clebber' (70).

There are five known outcrops of steatite in Shetland which we know to have been worked in Viking times: Clibberswick ('loom-weight-stone bay') in Unst, Strandibrough and Valhammars in Fetlar, Fethaland in the North Mainland and Catpund, Cunningsburgh in the South Mainland. (There are also a few other small, apparently unworked, outcrops of steatite in Shetland.) The largest of the Shetland sources was Catpund, where there are three substantial seams of steatite running in bands across the hillside above the cliffs at Cunningsburgh.

The Viking technique for making vessels was to chisel around the edge of a block of steatite which was roughly the shape and size of the finished vessel and then prise it off the live rockface. The artisan then chiselled the block into the required shape, inside and out. This made the block lighter to transport. If it broke during working, it would be abandoned. When one of the large pots broke, it was salvaged to make a smaller one. Sometimes the stone was either too faulted or the worker too inexperienced, and this second pot also broke. Finishing the pot and smoothing the surfaces were not done on the hill, but presumably back at the farm of the person who cut the stone. Archaeologists have never found evidence of a vessel-finishing workshop, but smoothing the surfaces would produce little more than dust which would blow away on the wind, an activity best carried out in the open air.

The shapes left when the vessels were removed can still be seen along Catpund Burn (71). The burn flows over some of the worked surfaces, and an area uncovered during excavations on the hillside has been fenced off for public viewing. The hill is covered in spoil-heaps, the debris of Viking quarrying. Beneath these, the whole hillside seems to have been worked, and there may even be quarry shafts to the south of the burn. Vessel shapes can also be seen in the rock at other sites, although most of these are on cliff faces and access is difficult, as indeed it must always have been.

Excavations at Catpund revealed wide variations in the methods of tooling the pots and in their shape and thickness, suggesting that large numbers of people were involved in quarrying. There may have been a degree of local

70 A steatite net-sinker and a handled vessel, both found at Jarlshof, demonstrate the versatility of the soft stone. (National Museums of Scotland)

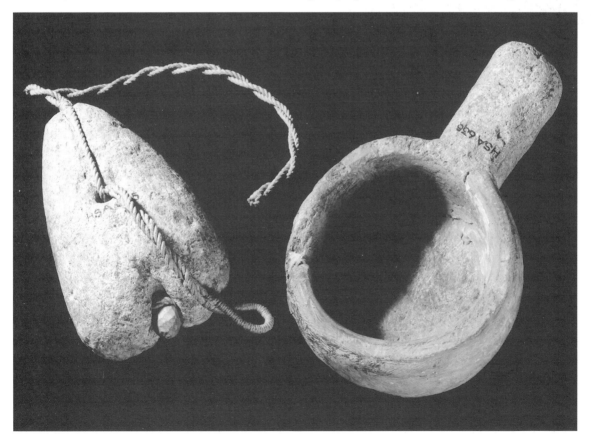

71 Catpund Viking quarries. (Joanna Richards)

organization; perhaps individual families had their own area of the quarry in the same way that Shetlanders have their own allotted peat bank today. By contrast, the Valhammars quarry in Fetlar seems to have been worked rather more systematically, in horizontal lines along the seams of a sea cliff. The Viking and Norse use of the quarries was so heavy it has obliterated all traces of the prehistoric workings.

'Thing' sites

The Vikings had a very ordered approach to the way their society worked and how they dealt with disputes and problems. Their Codes went into great detail about grazing sheep, who owed what if a sheep or a dog strayed, etc. They were, in essence, very fair and egalitarian, and intended to minimize infighting. In some areas of Shetland today udal law still affects land tenure, rights to the foreshore and rights of grazing in the 'scattald' (hill land).

Once the earldom of Orkney and Shetland was established, Shetland required a judicial and administrative centre together with a 'thing', or meeting-place, for the assembly. The Vikings choose a site at Tingwall, a fertile valley in the centre of Shetland Mainland. Tingwall had easy access to the harbour at Scalloway and was central for people travelling over land. There are two lochs in the centre of the Tingwall Valley, with a holm (islet) at the north-west end of the northerly loch attached to the mainland by a causeway of stepping stones, and originally the holm may have been used for duels. Other than the causeway, there are no visible structures on the holm, but there is evidence from the sixteenth century that it was part of the 'lawthing'. According to an account of 1701, people would wait beside the loch shore until individuals were called on to the holm in order to state their case. Although the holm was small, it would be a good vantage point from which to make pronouncements as sound travels well across water. The north-west shore of the loch is

flat, fertile land, which would have been convenient for pitching tents and tethering the horses of the people who travelled to the 'thing'. A round-towered church occupied a prominent position on the low hills to the north-west of the loch, in order to remind wrongdoers that they were answerable to God as well as the secular authorities!

By the end of the thirteenth century, Shetland was subdivided into regional 'thing districts'. Some of these are readily identifiable by their names: Sandsting, Aithsting, Nesting, Lunnasting and Delting. The regional assemblies dealt with matters which did not need to be dealt with at the principal 'thing' in Tingwall.

Viking burials

The first Viking settlers to die in Shetland were buried in pagan graves. A few of these have been found and identified by the objects which were buried with the bodies. Some Vikings were buried either in or under boats, and rivets were found at a largely unexcavated mound known as 'the Giant's Grave' at Aith in Fetlar. Viking boat burials may have been covered by oval mounds, possibly constructed with small stones or outlined with a kerb of stones set on end. Several possible boat burial sites have been identified, including Lunna, Lunnasting and Broadfoot, Foula. Other Viking burials might be visible as boat shapes outlined with stones, and there is a possible example of a family cemetery containing such graves at Belmont. All the proven Viking burials so far discovered in Shetland (and in Orkney too) have, however, had no visible indications above the ground, and were only discovered by chance.

Two graves found in Unst in the 1860s were identified as being female burials by the tortoise-shaped brooches which were found: items of women's jewellery. Such brooches were usually worn in pairs just below the collar bone as fastenings for cloaks. The brooches from Clibberswick (north Unst) were very worn; perhaps they were used by more than one generation before they were buried. They were accompanied by a bronze trefoil brooch, a silver armlet and two glass beads. The other Unst burial was identified by a tortoise-shaped brooch and a small circular bronze box (**72**). Other tortoise-shaped brooches have been found out of context in the south of Shetland, probably all originally from female burials. One such brooch, dated to the ninth century, has the imprint of tabby-weave cloth on the back, probably the material to which it had been pinned when it was buried.

In 1938, a ninth–tenth-century axe was found, together with some bones, in a stone-lined grave in the Christian burial ground at South Whiteness. This was either a fairly low-status male Viking burial (higher-status graves would normally contain more weaponry), or the burial of a Christian Viking who still felt the need to take some item of equipment to the grave for use in the after-life. This is one of several examples of the apparent integration of Pictish and Viking society evident at Christian sites. When the Vikings adopted Christianity, as they seem to have done by the second generation, they generally abandoned the

practice of placing objects in graves. As a result, Christian Viking graves cannot be distinguished from the burials of the native population.

Norse Christianity

Pagan Norse religion was not a proselytizing religion, and so the Vikings would have been unlikely to try to convert the Picts. Pagan burial customs may have died out within a generation, while Pictish religious centres not only continued in use but absorbed Norse influences (as seen in the Bressay Stone, for example).

In AD 995 Sigurd the Stout, Earl of Orkney and Shetland, chanced to meet Olaf Trygvason, King of Norway. According to the *Orkneyinga Saga*, Olaf threatened to kill Sigurd and his followers if they did not instantly convert to Christianity! As a result, Sigurd became a Christian along with his subjects in Orkney and Shetland. The sagas were written several centuries later in order to praise the deeds of the Vikings, and there may be little historical truth in this story. It would seem that pagan practices had all but died out by AD 900. Nevertheless, this may mark the point at which Shetland officially became Christian for, over the following decades, around 200 chapels sprang up, whether on the initiative of local groups or

72 Tortoise-shaped brooch from Unst (98.9mm (3.89in) long). (National Museums of Scotland)

families, or imposed as part of an unrecorded Shetland-wide plan. In some areas there seems to be a close correlation between the position of the chapels and the settlement districts called 'scattalds'. Each of the ten scattalds in Fetlar contained a chapel site. In AD 1030, Shetland fell under the aegis of the Bishop of Orkney. In each area one of the small chapels was eventually chosen to be the parish church.

Most of the chapels were small rectangular buildings, some of which had a rounded nave like that of the eleventh–twelfth-century chapel at St Ninian's. Others were more grand with a round tower at one end. These were later known as 'steeple kirks'. The round tower of St Laurence's Church at Papil stood until 1804. There were also 'steeple kirks' at Ireland (close to St Ninian's Isle), Tingwall and perhaps Sound

(south Lerwick); and the probable foundations of a fifth have recently been discovered on the island of Noss.

In 1994, excavations along the eroding cliff edge of the graveyard in Noss revealed what appeared to be the base of the round tower of a chapel, teetering on the edge. The tower was built of massive stones, faced on either side with flat slabs, and measured 2m (6ft) internally, with walls 1m (3ft) thick (73). This is similar in size to the base of the round tower still standing on the island of Egilsay in Orkney. If, as at Egilsay, the body of the chapel lay to the east, it will have already fallen into the sea. Although the area excavated in Noss was limited, a corner-post of a shrine, a carved cross (which

73 Probable round tower, Noss. (Val Turner)

Ian Fisher believes may be as early as seventh-century, although the style persisted for several centuries) and a rune stone were discovered, indicating an early date for the beginning of the site and continuous or repeated use of the burial ground until the nineteenth century. Noss may have potential for helping to unravel the development of Christianity in Shetland.

Monasteries

There are a number of potential monastic sites in Shetland which appear to date from around the twelfth century. The best Shetland example is Strandibrough, Fetlar, which has an 'Inner Brough', approached across a narrow isthmus, and an 'Outer Brough' which is now an islet. The Inner Brough has substantial earthworks across the isthmus on the landward side, and there are buildings on both broughs. Some of these are the shape and size of longhouses; others are smaller. The complex resembles a very large-scale Viking farmstead. Unlike the Pictish monastic sites, the land around the site at Strandibrough was good fertile land. There are only three sides visible on some of these buildings; possibly the fourth side was constructed of timber. There is no building identifiable as a chapel, but it is probable that as the focus of the monastic community, it would have been built in timber, the most prestigious material available for construction.

If the farm had belonged to an individual, its size indicates that it would have been owned by a person of considerable standing. If so, a peninsula was a strange place to site the farm buildings. The evidence suggests that the site was a self-sufficient monastic unit. Benedictine and Augustinian monasteries were being founded in Iceland and Greenland at this period, and the Shetland monasteries may have been of these orders. Raymond Lamb has suggested that these sites may be the monasteries of the same communities who had previously lived on the more austere stack-tops and were now being rather more realistic (see Chapter 9). It is possible to imagine that a community on The

Clett would find life easier at nearby Strandibrough.

The islet of Brei Holm, off Papa Stour, contains seven buildings, the largest of which looks like a longhouse. Maiden Stack, also off Papa Stour, supports a single longhouse building. In 1822, Hibbert recorded the story that the house on the Maiden Stack was inhabited by a woman who took vows of chastity. She allegedly abandoned her vows when a man managed to scale the cliffs of the stack. The site may well have been a nunnery, probably housing several women. There are other stories in Papa Stour which claim that these sites were leper colonies, like some of the other ruins on the hillside in Papa Stour. The leper story is unconvincing because lepers usually lived in places which were relatively accessible from centres of habitation, so that the inhabitants could collect food left out for them by their relatives.

The Norse mill

The Norse mill was so called because it was introduced into Shetland during the Norse period, although not necessarily by the Scandinavian settlers. In Shetland today the Norse mill is more commonly known as the 'horizontal mill', (**colour plates 14 (a) and (b)**). The mills were small, water-powered rotary querns, the upper stone being turned by a shaft attached to angled paddles in the underhouse below. Water was usually diverted from the burn when required by a system of leats.

Horizontal mills were found in classical Greece, early China and Tibet, and the idea gradually spread, reaching Ireland by the seventh century AD at the latest. It is possible that the concept of the mill travelled from Ireland to Scandinavia via Shetland, rather than the reverse. Norse settlers were, however, clearly familiar with horizontal mills. The earliest one discovered in the Northern Isles, dating from the eleventh–twelfth centuries, is at Orphir, in Orkney; the first evidence for horizontal milling in Shetland comes from toy millstones found during the excavation of Norse sites, including

Belmont, Unst. These miniature steatite querns each have a rectangular notch near the central hole which, in a working mill, would connect the topstone to the drive-shaft.

By the eighteenth century there were large numbers of horizontal mills, of standard shapes and sizes, throughout Shetland. There were as many as eight mills along one burn (for example, Clumlie, South Mainland). The water was often dammed prior to use, and the crofters would all go to their respective mills at the appointed hour. When everything was ready, the sluice was opened and the burn diverted, via leats, through each mill in turn. The crofters worked day and night until the job was completed or the water exhausted. It was a time associated with merriment, and there are several Shetland fiddle tunes concerning milling and the trows (Shetland trolls) who allegedly visited the millers while they worked through the night! Horizontal mills were fundamental to crofting life until this century, when they were largely superseded by vertical mills.

Several horizontal mills have been restored throughout Shetland, including a series at

74 Noosts in use at Scatness during the 1930s. (J. R. C. Hamilton)

Huxter, Sandness, one at Burraland in Trondra (where the oldest surviving plants, bere and black oats, are still grown, providing grist for the mill and thatch for the roof), and one at the Croft House Museum, in the South Mainland.

Noosts

Noosts were another Norse innovation which continued in use until recent times. A noost is a boat-shaped hollow, dug into the bank above an area of beach or a slipway, into which a boat can be pulled from the shore. The noost fitted the boat snugly, providing shelter from wind, which even in recent times has lifted an unsecured boat over the roof of a house! The noost may have been protected by a stone revetment and stone-lined, making it more resistant to erosion. Noosts may be found singly or in groups. In some cases there are two sets: an upper set for winter use when the seas were rougher and potentially higher, and a lower one for more regular summer use (**74**).

Most of the noosts which survive are probably post-medieval. They are long and narrow and would have accommodated a variety of clinker-built boats (foureens, sixareens, Ness Yoals, etc.), all adapted from Viking boat-building techniques to suit the Shetland waters. Viking and Norse noosts would have been vulnerable to coastal erosion and the rising sea level. Many of the noosts which survive in Scandinavia are bigger than the Shetland ones; perhaps Shetland once boasted larger noosts to accommodate the longships of the Viking settlers, as well as smaller ones for the boats used in coastal waters.

Although Shetland gradually evolved into a Scottish crofting economy, the Viking impact on Shetland was as permanent as it was dramatic. Shetland annually remembers its Viking past in the Victorian fire festival of Up Helly Aa. Many of the street names (King Harald Street, St Olaf Street, St Sunniva Street, etc.), the retention of a Norse element in the dialect, property which is still held udally, and the stained glass in the Town Hall (built in 1882) all evoke saga times. Shetland has a distinctive sense of place, strongly linked to a sense of the past.

11
Looking forward to the past

Archaeological techniques are advancing rapidly, and what we currently believe to be true may well be overturned in the fullness of time, in the light of new discoveries. Shetland is fortunate to be attracting the attention of many of the archaeologists at the cutting edge of archaeological science and theory. As a result, our understanding of ancient Shetland is increasing year by year.

Perhaps the most exciting project currently underway is a collaborative venture between Shetland Amenity Trust and the University of Bradford, who are excavating at Old Scatness Broch, and surveying the surrounding area (**colour plate 15**). One of the original aims of the project was to excavate a previously undisturbed broch site, which was buried in earth and sand to a height of at least 5m (16ft). As such, it is among the twenty most complete examples of brochs in Scotland. The other aim was to examine the surrounding area, in order to ascertain how the broch functioned in relation to other sites in the vicinity.

Old Scatness includes remains from the crofting period dating back to at least the Bronze Age, and has proved to be rich in environmental remains (charred plant, macroplant, animal and fish bones, insect and snail remains). One aspect of the project is to examine the environmental remains from the crofting period and compare these against the documentary evidence, which should help us to discover the limitations of the archaeological evidence. From this it will be

possible to work backwards in order to arrive at a greater understanding of what the evidence from the Iron Age levels might mean. Jarlshof was excavated before archaeologists appreciated how much information was held in environmental evidence, let alone how to retrieve much of it, and so the excavation at Old Scatness will go a long way in furthering our knowledge about the social, agricultural and industrial economy of both Jarlshof itself and ancient Shetland as a whole (**75**).

The results of the excavation have exceeded expectations. The broch is surrounded by a

75 Excavation of a horse, buried during the crofting period at Old Scatness. (Shetland Amenity Trust)

village containing a wide variety of types of building, each standing at least one storey high. The village includes a building with its corbelled roof still in place: this is probably the most complete Iron Age house in Britain, affording unprecedented opportunities to examine the roof structure. The excavation of the village, which includes wheelhouses and various cellular buildings, will allow archaeologists to establish the sequence of different building styles, which will in turn shed light on other buildings within Shetland.

The team are using the most sophisticated dating techniques available in order to refine the dating of the different aspects of the site. It has been customary to get an idea of the broad date of a site from the pottery and objects found, to establish the sequence of events by stratigraphy, and to hope to find sufficient organic material to gain some radiocarbon dates for the site. Today, it is possible to get a more accurate radiocarbon date using a smaller amount of organic matter by accelerator dating. This is being combined at Old Scatness with archaeo-magnetic dating, a method for dating hearths and burnt objects which are *in situ*.

Thermoluminescence (for pottery) and dendrochronology (for wood) are additional dating methods which can be employed if suitable material is found. Not only will we arrive at a good dating sequence for Iron Age buildings, but we will also be able to pin down the dating of pottery and objects more firmly, which in turn will help us to date some of the

phases of Jarlshof and other Iron Age sites in Shetland more precisely.

Topographical survey is being used in order to record the visible remains of all periods, whilst soil micromorphology is providing information about how soils were created. Geophysics is giving us information about what may lie under the soil in areas which we have no immediate plans to excavate, and building pseudo-sections from the results of such surveys allows us a three-dimensional preview. In the laboratory, residue analysis will investigate what was being cooked in some of the pots and bowls. Demonstrators are experimenting in copying objects found on the site using Iron Age technology and materials, and have been testing the effectiveness of different fuels by measuring the temperatures given off within a replica Pictish hearth.

Combining all this research with specialist studies of all the categories of environmental remains, the more conventional artefact analysis, and the investigation of industrial debris, we find ourselves inundated with new information which will have an enormous impact on our thinking about ancient Shetland. Noel Fojut, a Principal Inspector of Ancient Monuments with Historic Scotland, has described Old Scatness as having 'a greater potential to expand our knowledge of Iron Age archaeology than any other site currently under excavation'. The implications for Shetland itself are enormous, and the future for the past is tremendously exciting.

Places to visit

Most of Shetland's archaeological sites are situated on croft land. As a general rule the public are welcome to walk anywhere in the islands as long as they do no damage and shut any gates which they open; however, please observe 'No dogs' signs. Dogs must always be kept on a lead, even on hill land, and never taken amongst sheep during lambing (May/June). Some of the sites are a long way from the road and you would be well advised to take the relevant 1:25,000 Ordnance Survey map and a compass with you. Sites marked with an asterisk have been/are to be interpreted for visitors at the site.

Shetland Mainland

Catpund Burn, Cunningsburgh (HU 423271)
Steatite quarries; the visible remains are primarily Viking/Norse extending up the burn and south of it. (Follow the burn to reach a fenced-off area of the quarry floor exposed by excavation.)

Clickhimin, Lerwick (HU 464408)
Bronze Age village, blockhouse fort and broch with wheelhouse remains inside. Excavated and standing several metres high, on the outskirts of Lerwick (Historic Scotland).

Culswick, West Side (HU 253448)
Striking remains of broch built with angular red sandstone blocks, standing *c.* 4m (13ft) high, with an unusual triangular door lintel. It is

possible to make out some of the internal features (about a mile west-north-west from the end of the Culswick road).

Giant's Grave, North Roe (HU 361854)
Two chambered cairns, one completely scattered except for the two large terminal orthostats of the 'Giant's Grave' (west of the A970).

Gruting School (HU 282498)
A group of oval houses – the best is situated on the hill slope, a second is visible underneath a small garage, and a third is cut through by the road.

Houlland, Eshaness (HU 213791)
A broch standing about 2m (7ft) high, on a promontory projecting into the loch. The remains of several buildings surround the foot of the broch – some may be contemporary, but others are clearly later. A gentle, but scenic, walk about 500m (1640ft) north of the Eshaness lighthouse.

Huxter, West Side (HU 172571)
Three horizontal mills which have been restored, situated on the burn, beside the sea at the end of the Huxter road.

Jarlshof, Dunrossness (HU 398095)
Bronze Age village, broch, wheelhouses and other Iron Age remains, Viking and Norse (largely continuous occupation ending with a sixteenth-century Laird's House). One of the best

sites in Britain. Entrance from Sumburgh Hotel car park (Historic Scotland – admission charge).

Kirk Holm, Sand (HU 337460)
Monastic site, with a row of buildings on an islet. In the voe to the east of the road to Reawick.

*Lawting Holm, Tingwall (HU 418434)
Site of the Norse Parliament, situated on a knoll within the loch (north end of Tingwall Loch).

March Cairn, Eshaness (HU 221789)
Unusual square-chambered cairn. (Follow track from Priesthoulland, then bear off to the right along a fence.)

*Ness of Burgi, Dunrossness (HU 388086)
Impressive excavated promontory fort in spectacular position (1km (half a mile) south of the Scat Ness road end; gentle walk followed by a short, more rocky, walk).

Ness of Sound, Lerwick (HU 471390)
Burnt mound on farm land.

*Old Scatness, Dunrossness (HU 389106)
Broch site and Iron Age village, with houses standing full height. Under excavation until 2000 (visitors welcome), after which on permanent display. As exciting as Jarlshof.

Punds Water, Central Mainland (HU 324712)
One of Shetland's best-preserved heel-shaped cairns with a very clear, and accessible, cruciform chamber in the centre. Rough walking from Mangaster road (map and compass).

Ronas Hill, Northmavine (HU 305834)
Scotland's highest chambered cairn: it survives well, although with some twentieth-century modification! Walk from the top of Collafirth Hill (map and compass).

*Stanydale, West Side (HU 285502)
Prehistoric 'temple' and three oval house sites,

amongst fragments of walling (signposted across moor from enlarged lay-by. Historic Scotland).

*Scord of Brouster, West Side (HU 255516)
Excavated Neolithic/Bronze Age farmstead: three house sites and associated fields and clearance cairns clearly visible. Also a later ring cairn (signposted from lay-by).

Shetland – islands

*Bayanne, Sellafirth, Yell (HU 977519)
Well preserved, excavated Iron Age house site. (Leave main road to Gutcher to follow track to Bayanne House, and follow signs).

Boardastubble, Unst (HP 578034)
Possibly the largest standing stone in Shetland, 3.6m (12ft) high, made of a gneiss boulder (situated beside the track to Lund).

*Belmont, Unst (HU 568007)
Viking/Norse house site under excavation and Bronze Age cup-marked rocks adjacent. (Climb hillslope above the main road north at the Belmont junction. Interpretation to follow excavation.)

Birrier of West Sandwick, Yell (HU 438913)
Two rows of small dwellings, thought to be a monastic site (north-west of track to Birriesgirt – almost inaccessible, but view from the cliff to the south, or better still, from the air).

Blue Mull, Unst (HP 557045)
Monastic buildings? A line of seven rectangular buildings situated on a headland. (Follow the coast north from Westing via the early chapel site and circular enclosure at Kirkaby.)

Burgi Geos, Yell (HP 478034)
Promontory fort, with blockhouse and *chevaux de frise* in spectacular situation. (Walk from track beside Gloup Voe, then head south-west across peaty moor. Map and compass are essential.)

Funzie Girt Dyke, Fetlar (HU 616930–626945)
Substantial prehistoric land division crossing
Fetlar north–south.

Haltadans, Fetlar (HU 618928)
Probable Bronze Age cremation cemetery, a
circle 11m (36ft) diameter, bounded by twenty-
three stones, with two central upright stones.

*Hamar, Unst (HP 646094)
Single-period Norse house, described as the best
example of a rural longhouse known in
Scotland, to be excavated and interpreted. (Walk
from either Little Hamar or Keen of Hamar.)

Landberg, Fair Isle (HZ 222722)
Iron Age promontory fort, partially excavated
1996/7. Impressive ramparts, and building
behind (south of North Haven).

*Mousa (HU 457236)
At just over 13m (43ft), Scotland's best-preserved
Iron Agebroch site. It is still possible to climb the
staircase to the wall-head. The interior floor area
was altered significantly in the late Iron Age (boat,
by arrangement, from Sand Lodge pier, Sandwick).

Gungstie, Noss (HU 539401)
Graveyard in use for over 1000 years, from the
seventh century. Foundations of probable round
tower excavated. Corner-post, rune stone and
early cross-slab also found on the site (by boat,
seasonally, from Bressay).

St Ninian's Isle, South Mainland (HU 368209)
Site of sixth-century chapel, with remains of
twelfth-century one above it. Excavations in the
late 1950s revealed Iron Age cist burials, Pictish
corner-post shrines and the famous St Ninian's
Isle Treasure. (Signposted from Bigton; walk
across the tombolo. The tombolo may be
covered by sea during bad winter weather.)

St Olaf's Kirk, Unst (HP 566040)
Twelfth-century chapel still standing, although
the east end has been rebuilt. The lintel over the

east window incorporates a stone which has had
a fish incised into it, thought to be a Pictish
symbol stone reused. (Drive or walk (it is a long
walk) to the end of the track to Lund.)

Pettigarth's Field, Whalsay (centred around
HU 587652)
Two excellent examples of prehistoric houses
(the Benie Hoose and the 'Standing Stones of
Yoxie') situated below two chambered cairns,
one square, the other round. (Walk 1km (1 /2
miles) north-east from Isbister – all the fences
contain gates. Map and compass.)

South Harbour, Fair Isle (HZ 2006998)
An impressive set of summer noosts situated on
the shore line, having a winter set in the banks
above them (east of road to Puffin).

Underhoull, Unst (HP 573043)
Impressive unexcavated broch with massive
ramparts, situated above a Norse house site
excavated in the late 1950s. House site cut
through an Iron Age souterrain which is still
visible. (The broch is beside the road to
Westing; the house site is situated on more level
ground in the field below.)

Vementry (HU 295609)
Neolithic heel-shaped cairn in excellent
condition, with curving façade of stones over 1m
(3ft) high (boat by arrangement from Vementry
Farm. Compass and map recommended).

Windhouse, Yell (HU 488919)
Unexcavated sites below the 'haunted house'
include a broch mound, a Viking/Norse house
and a small, but well-preserved, chambered
cairn (HU 487917).

Museums
Many areas of Shetland have local museums
which interpret their immediate area. The
principal archaeological collection is, however,
held at the **Shetland Museum**, Hillhead, Lerwick.

The collection includes the finds from the excavations at Clickhimin, the Scord of Brouster, the Sumburgh cist and Kebister and the Mail Stone, as well as replicas of the St Ninian's Isle Treasure. The Shetland Museum regularly includes temporary exhibitions of archaeological work in progress, including finds from sites under excavation. The Museum is open daily except on Sundays and public holidays. The majority of Shetland's carved stones (primarily Pictish) are held at the **National Museums of Scotland** in Chambers Street, Edinburgh.

Local museums which often include archaeological exhibits are:
Fetlar Interpretive Centre; Unst Heritage Centre (Haroldswick); The Old Haa, Burravoe, Yell; Tangwick Haa, Eshaness; Bressay Interpretive Centre (restricted opening hours); George Walterson Memorial Centre, Fair Isle (admission by arrangement). The Warp and Weft Cafe, Hoswick, also mounts displays about archaeology.

The **Shetland Sites and Monuments Record** stores information about the known sites in Shetland, and information from it can be obtained by appointment. (Telephone the Shetland Amenity Trust.) The Trust is always pleased to receive reports of newly discovered sites.

Further reading

Guide books/young people

Ashmore, Patrick *Jarlshof: A Walk through the Past.* HMSO, Edinburgh, 1993.

Fojut, N. *A Guide to Prehistoric and Viking Shetland.* Shetland Times, Lerwick, 1993.

Fojut, N. and Pringle, R. D. *The Ancient Monuments of Shetland.* HMSO, Edinburgh, 1993.

Ritchie, A. *Shetland: Exploring Scotland's Heritage.* HMSO, Edinburgh, 1997.

Turner, Val *How to be a Detective.* Past Books, Lerwick, 1993.

Detailed reading

Buckley V. *Burnt Offerings.* Wordwell Ltd, Dublin, 1990.

Forsyth, K. 'Language in Pictland, spoken and written' in E. Nicoll (ed.), *A Pictish Panorama.* Balgavies, 1995.

Foster, Sally *Picts, Gaels and Scots.* Batsford, London, 1996.

Henshall, A. S. *The Chambered Tombs of Scotland*, Vols 1 and 2. Edinburgh University Press, Edinburgh, 1993.

Hunter, John *Fair Isle: The Archaeology of an Island Community.* HMSO, Edinburgh, 1996.

Lamb, R. G. *Iron Age Promontory Forts in the Northern Isles.* BAR, Oxford, 1980.

Low, George *A Tour through Orkney and Schetland 1774.* Facsimile, Bookmag, Inverness 1979.

Ritchie, Anna *Viking Scotland.* Batsford, London, 1993.

Smith, B. (ed.) *Shetland Archaeology.* Shetland Times, Lerwick, 1985.

Turner, Val (ed.) *The Shaping of Shetland.* Shetland Times, Lerwick, 1998.

Waugh, Doreen *Shetland's Northern Links: Language and History.* Shetland Times, Lerwick, 1996.

Excavation reports

Downes, Jane and Lamb, Raymond *Sumburgh* (forthcoming)

Hamilton, J. R. C. *Excavations at Jarlshof, Shetland.* HMSO, Edinburgh, 1956.

Hamilton, J. R. C. *Excavations at Clickhimin, Shetland.* HMSO, Edinburgh, 1968.

Owen, Olwyn *Kebister.* Society of Antiquaries, Edinburgh (forthcoming)

Sharples, Niall *Upper Scalloway.* Oxbow, Oxford (forthcoming)

Whittle, Alasdair *Scord of Brouster: An Early Agricultural Settlement in Shetland.* Oxbow, Oxford, 1986.

The *Proceedings of the Society of Antiquaries of Scotland* contains a number of important reports, including:

Calder, C. S. T. 1955–6 *Stone Age House Sites in Shetland.* vol. 89

Calder, C. S. T. 1962–3 *Cairns, Neolithic Houses and Burnt Mounds in Shetland.* vol. 96

Carter, Stephen *et al. The Iron Age in Shetland: Excavations at Five Sites Threatened by Coastal Erosion.* vol. 125, 1995.

Fojut, Noel *Is Mousa a Broch?* vol. 111, 1981.

Small, Alan 1946–66 *Excavations at Underhoull, Unst, Shetland.* vol. 98

Turner, Val *The Mail Stone: An Incised Pictish Figure from Mail, Shetland.* vol. 124, 1994.

Index

(Page numbers in **bold** refer to illustrations)

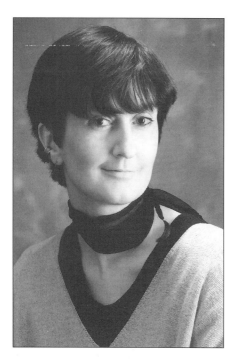

The author

Val Turner has held the post of Shetland Archaeologist since it was created in 1986. With first and second degrees from the University of Birmingham, she is currently an Honorary Research Fellow in the Department of Archaeological Sciences, University of Bradford. She has written a wide range of papers and articles about many aspects of Shetland Archaeology, including a children's introduction, 'How to be a Detective'. Val is committed to 'giving archaeology back to the people it belongs to'. This ethos underlies the 'Old Scatness Broch and Jarlshof Environs Project', probably Scotland's biggest and most exciting excavation, survey and heritage project currently in progress, set up by Val with colleagues in the Shetland Amenity Trust.